George Eliot's *Middlemarch*, first published in 1872, is of central importance in the history of English literature and one of the few undeniably great nineteenth-century English novels.

This book is a collection of original critical essays, employing a variety of approaches, yet complementary in perspective, which shed new light on a number of aspects of the novel, especially on its structure and on its approach to character.

The authors of the papers, Barbara Hardy, Gordon Haight, U.C. Knoepflmacher, David Carroll, and Gillian Beer, are well known for their individual contributions to the study of English literature.

All five papers are written at a high level of critical adventurousness, and the editor's introduction locates them in the framework of contemporary work on George Eliot. This volume is an important contribution not only to the study of George Eliot, but to that of the novel as well.

Ian Adam, a member of the department of English at the university of Calgary, has published several articles on *Middlemarch*, and written an introductory book on George Eliot. He is at present working on a book on Eliot's major novels.

EDITED BY IAN ADAM

THIS
PARTICULAR
WEB

Essays on *Middlemarch*

PUBLISHED IN ASSOCIATION WITH
THE FACULTY OF ARTS AND SCIENCE OF
THE UNIVERSITY OF CALGARY BY
UNIVERSITY OF TORONTO PRESS
TORONTO AND BUFFALO

© University of Toronto Press 1975
Toronto and Buffalo
Printed in Canada

Library of Congress Cataloging in Publication Data
Main entry under title:

This particular web.

Includes index.
CONTENTS: Hardy, B. Middlemarch and the passions — Haight, G.S.
George Eliot's 'eminent failure,' Will Ladislaw — Knoepflmacher, U.C.
Fusing fact and myth: the new reality of Middlemarch [etc]

1 Eliot, George, pseud., i.e. Marian Evans, afterwards Cross, 1819-1880
Middlemarch. I. Adam, Ian.
PR 4662.T48   823'.8   75-15844
ISBN 0-8020-5332-7

'I at least have so much to do in unravelling certain human lots, and seeing
how they are woven and interwoven, that all the light I can command
must be concentrated on this particular web, and not dispersed over that
tempting range of relevancies called the universe.' (15:105)

Contents

Contributors

GILLIAN BEER university lecturer, Cambridge university, and fellow of Girton college, Cambridge. She is the author of *Meredith: A Change of Masks* (1970) and *The Romance* (1970).

DAVID CARROLL reader in English at the university of Lancaster. He is the author of *Chinua Achebe* (1970) and editor of *George Eliot: The Critical Heritage* (1971).

GORDON S. HAIGHT professor emeritus of English literature at Yale university. He is the author of *George Eliot and John Chapman* (1940, 1969), *George Eliot: A Biography* (1968), and editor of *The George Eliot Letters* (1953-4), *Adam Bede* (1948), *Middlemarch* (1956), and *The Mill on the Floss* (1962). He is general editor of the Clarendon George Eliot, now in preparation.

BARBARA HARDY professor of English, Birkbeck college, university of London. She is the author of *The Novels of George Eliot* (1959), *The Appropriate Form* (1964), *The Moral Art of Dickens* (1970), *The Exposure of Luxury: Radical Themes in Thackeray* (1972), and the editor of two collections of essays on George Eliot: *Middlemarch* (1967) and *Critical Essays on George Eliot* (1970). To be published in 1975 are 'Tellers and Listeners: The Narrative Imagination,' and 'A Study of Jane Austen.'

U.C. KNOEPFLMACHER professor of English, university of California, Berkeley. He is the author of *Religious Humanism and the Victorian Novel* (1965), *George Eliot's Early Novels: The Limits of Realism* (1968), and *Laughter and Despair: Readings in Ten Novels of the Victorian Era* (1971).

Introduction

This book gathers papers presented in commemoration of the centenary of the publication of George Eliot's *Middlemarch*, a work which, in Geoffrey Tillotson's words, might be overrated only by saying 'that it was easily the best of the half-dozen best novels of the world.'[1] Four of the papers, by Gordon Haight, U.C. Knoepflmacher, Barbara Hardy, and David Carroll, were presented at a conference held in Calgary, Canada, in 1971, while a fifth, by Gillian Beer, was given at a conference held in Leicester, England, in 1972. In introduction I should state that they represent an effort to pay tribute to *Middlemarch* through the work of scholars of varying critical approach, united only by their intense interest in the novel. But no one would expect the results of such an exercise to be entirely random, and what has emerged is a collection with some lively junctures of method and concern. Sometimes these are of opinions which conflict in a manner that can only be seen as healthy for criticism; more frequently the views are complementary. For example, different sources for Dorothea's name are discussed by two of the authors, but the explanations do not exclude each other. The authors of the papers do not presume *Middlemarch* to be an inexhaustible 'Sacred Book,' but their studies nevertheless show how varied critical methods may open different veins of richness in the work, and even in identical parts of it.

One common concern is with character. We now seem to be past the time when the study of character was regarded as a regression to discredited and unscientific nineteenth-century practice, and was to be conducted, when done at all, defensively or apologetically. And while, as Barbara Hardy points out elsewhere,[2] such a phenomenon has been especially evident in the critical history of novelists other than George Eliot, whose overriding humane interests compel our attention, debate over character as a theoretical issue was not long ago vigorous indeed. I mention this fact in order to introduce the name of a scholar and critic explicitly and frequently referred to in the papers and in discussion at the Calgary conference: the late W.J. Harvey who, some six years before its proceedings, felt the need, at that point in critical history, to write a defence of character in his *Character and the Novel* (London 1965). He traced the 'retreat from character' and the 'attack on character' to their origins in Shakespearean criticism, and the effect of his research was to place these movements as part of the history of criticism. The frequent discussion of character in these papers must be seen as one of several tributes to his work and influence.

It is noteworthy that, where character is discussed, the focus seems to be especially on Will Ladislaw and Dorothea, though it is by no means exclusively so. With the exception of members of the Garth circle, every major character receives extended treatment at some point in the papers. But Will and Dorothea receive substantial treatment in virtually all, Will indeed being the main subject of one. The attention may indicate the perennial interest in these characters as representative of the 'problem' areas in George Eliot, those love relationships in which her heroines' idealism and sexuality seem to fuse, bringing critical objections of authorial identification. But only two of the papers, by Gordon Haight and Barbara Hardy, deal with the 'problem' as a problem. The studies of Dorothea by Gillian Beer, U.C. Knoepflmacher, and David Carroll treat her in different ways as an embodiment of other kinds of forces in George Eliot's imagination, and among these studies only that of Gillian Beer deals specifically with the relationship between Will and Dorothea. Among the other characters discussed Casaubon, Lydgate, and Rosamond receive considerable attention, but perhaps one should make special mention here of David Carroll's revaluation of Raffles, the nemesis of Bulstrode. Surely this brilliant, jeering character will never again be perceived as merely 'melodramatic'.[3]

Both Gordon Haight and Barbara Hardy deal with evaluative issues raised in George Eliot's presentation of character, though in Barbara Hardy's case these are subordinate to another concern. Gordon Haight concentrates on Will Ladislaw as a character and as the hero of the novel. With a wide-ranging scholarship which draws on the novel's critical reception, its reading public, and on an intimate knowledge of novelistic convention and of the text, he conducts a lively defence of Will against his detractors. These have not been wanting, and Leslie Stephen's statement that Will is 'almost obtrusively a favourite with his creator' may be taken as representative of comments which have been repeated frequently, albeit with variations, in the criticism. One of the main defences against such charges of authorial indulgence has to rest upon evidence of authorial irony, and Gordon Haight's study is in good part composed of a demonstration of its abundance and centrality. But there are other important points in his case, raised, for example, in discussion of Will's precise social standing in the novel and the traditional inheritance of property in English novels. Barbara Hardy's final assessment of Will perhaps conforms more to the orthodox estimate, but she argues its limitations as much as its degree of justice. Her general concern with the 'charting of the passions' leads naturally to a consideration of Will, that character about whom it is often asserted the author is too passionate. What emerges is another insight into authorial irony, with Will, much more than the author, shown as confused and deceived about feeling.

Barbara Hardy's paper differs from that of Gordon Haight in that it especially examines an aspect of character, the emotional life. George Eliot's relation to Wordsworth may be mentioned here, for the Marian Evans who wrote to Maria Lewis in 1839 that in Wordsworth she 'never before met with so many of my own feelings, expressed just as I could [wish] ... them' (*Letters* I 34), continued, throughout her career, to feel such an affinity and to embody it in her writings. For Wordsworth, as for George Eliot, the enlargement of the sympathies was the aim of both art and human development. Both authors saw one means of such enlargement in attention to the feelings of fictional characters, but George Eliot, in the course of her development, shifts her attention (though by no means in a schematic manner) from 'commonplace people,'[4] related to Wordsworth's primitives, to more complex and sophisticated figures whose psychology has affinities with that of Wordsworth himself. He presents his own development in *The Prelude* with a close attention to moral and spiritual issues, and George Eliot shows similar concern in presenting the inner lives of the characters in *Middlemarch*. Barbara Hardy studies especially her treatment of the *relations* of feelings: those between author and characters, between character and character, and not least between different and conflicting feelings within character. There is, in her paper, the ghost of a structural analysis, for the relations examined at times assume the patterning of form. Both Will and Casaubon are shown as let down by literary expectations, and Dorothea and Casaubon, in another parallel, are shown as moved, in great crises in their lives, out of what George Eliot terms a 'persistent self.' But it would be misleading to state that form in such a sense is primarily suggested by the paper: the preoccupation is with George Eliot's extraordinary sensitivity to subtleties of feeling expressed in the course of the ordinary lives of her characters. The form traced is as much contour as figure in the carpet.

Henry James, speaking of the intellectual qualities of *Middlemarch* in his famous review in *Galaxy*, wrote that it 'denotes a mind in which imagination is illumined by faculties rarely found in fellowship with it." George Eliot's long intellectual apprenticeship as a scholar, editor, and translator left its impress on all her work, but perhaps especially on the later novels, and in different ways David Carroll, Gillian Beer, and U.C. Knoepflmacher concern themselves with it. The history of the criticism shows that such studies have been often (and quite naturally) occupied with George Eliot's place in the history of ideas, so it is worth mentioning that in these papers there is less attention to the ideas as ideas than to their 'incarnation' (to use George Eliot's term) in her prose. But where David Carroll focuses on a philosophical problem which engages her in *Middlemarch* and demonstrates how it is embodied in its action and in the relations among its characters, Gillian Beer deals with a dilemma embedded in *The Lifted Veil*, a tale written some sixteen years earlier, and shows its resolution in the structure of the novel. The latter part of her paper traces a major source of this resolution in the author's reading of Christian myth and assumes affinities with U.C.

Knoepflmacher's study. It too is concerned with George Eliot's reading, tracing her 'incarnation' of history and myth in the novel.

Of the three papers, that of David Carroll comes closest to Barbara Hardy's. He too studies characters let down by expectations, focuses sharply on action, and makes us aware of a patterning of human relations. But he deals less with the characters' emotional lives than with their ways of interpreting the world. The theme which underlies George Eliot's presentation of those ways is epistemological: to what extent are our perceptions a reflection of our desires, and to what extent are they objectively valid? This question has echoes in much human experience, recorded and unrecorded, but it is perhaps especially a nineteenth-century question. It underlies the 'Immortality Ode' and Coleridge's 'Dejection.' In the *Biographia Literaria*, chapter XII, it is the source of speculation on the relations between 'subject' and 'object.' It would also seem to be related to the Victorian crisis of religious belief, for here, too, an uneasy mediation between an anthropomorphic view of nature and an 'objective' one is recorded by writers as various as Carlyle, Tennyson, Arnold, and George Eliot herself.

In an unrevised posthumous essay, W.J. Harvey studied George Eliot's concept of nature, and defined the term in her usage as 'an icon of the mysterious complexity of things.'[5] David Carroll also examines the mysterious complexity of nature as seen by George Eliot and by her characters and especially one facet of that complexity, its comprehension of humanity. The characters must face not only the difficult task of interpreting the passive material world, but also that of understanding other characters, who are active, and have ideas and interpretations of their own. Quite clearly such engagements may lead to error, conflict, and disenchantment, yet they may also yield victories of truth, conciliation, and transfiguration. David Carroll underlines the characters' perceptions as above all *generative* of such consequences and shows the novelist at crucial points associating them with the demonology and angelology of the Gothic novel. We are led from George Eliot's concern with a highly abstract question to the 'monsters' and 'miracles' of *Middlemarch.*

Gillian Beer deals less with the characters' relations to each other than with their creator's relation to them. It is generally acknowledged that George Eliot's portrayal of character reflects a major thesis in her ethical doctrine, that genuine altruism is a human possibility. Many central characters are finally motivated by sympathy, their selfless acts generating similar acts in others. Yet in that curious work, *The Lifted Veil*, George Eliot appears to deny the possibility of such motive. Its hero, Latimer, is cursed with prescience and omniscience which enables him to discern the final reality of friends and family and to find it indeed shallow, selfish, and unredeemable. Mrs Beer argues *The Lifted Veil* as a fictional manifestation of one of those collapses of confidence to which George Eliot was subject throughout her life. She traces her escape from depressive vision through her recognition in *Middlemarch* of human reality as extraordinarily complex and ultimately irreducible. That recognition is implicit in the 'latency' of her creations, a phenomenon particularly explored in a highly concentrated focus on allusions in the conversations between Dorothea and Ladislaw in Rome.

One of the ways in which George Eliot's reading leaves its mark on *Middlemarch* is in such allusions. They may be not necessarily direct allusions to authors or works, but oblique ones to concept; they may not always be immediately recognizable to the reader. Her contemporary, R.H. Hutton, complained, in his *Spectator* review of book I of *Middlemarch*, that the ordinary reader might not catch the reference to 'Professor Tyndall's speculations as to the cause of the blueness of the sky' in George Eliot's comment on young Dorothea's tendency to interpret 'signs' with 'wonder, hope, belief, vast as the sky, and coloured by a diffused thimbleful of matter in the shape of knowledge,' yet the reference, once noted, sheds light on the passage in making the word 'coloured' a scientific, indeed 'metaphysical' image. The main task of U.C. Knoepflmacher's paper is to indicate the sources of similar allusions in *Middlemarch*, and through such indication illuminate both the passages in which they occur and the novel as a whole. He takes only four key references from the novel but by tracing their origins in George Eliot's reading down to the faintest echoes is able to give us a sense of the rich associative imagination of the author. He takes as his sub-title 'The New Reality of *Middlemarch*,' and opens the question of her changing realism, no longer the close portrayal of tangible reality seen in the early novels.

All the participants see 'new reality' beyond the tangible in *Middle-march.* If for U.C. Knoepflmacher it is a network of allusions dense, complex and systematic, for Barbara Hardy it is an equally complex and more tangled world of feeling. For David Carroll it is a philosophical question, one dealing with the grounds of knowledge, which charges action in the novel. Gordon Haight sees it revealed especially in ironic treatment of the psychology of her characters. Gillian Beer finds it in the suggestiveness of their rendering, reflecting George Eliot's hard-earned recognition of humanity's 'penetralium of mystery.' There are many 'realities' in *Middlemarch,* but all who contemplate it here also perceive an underlying unity in the mind of the author, compassionate, subtle, ironic, earnest, informed, humane.

All citations from *Middlemarch* are to the Riverside edition (Boston 1956), and consist of the chapter number and page number separated by a colon. Citations from other works by George Eliot are to the Cabinet edition (Edinburgh 1878-80) and follow the same form.

Publication of this work is made possible by grants from the Humanities Research Council of Canada, using funds supplied by the Canada Council, and from the Faculty of Arts and Science, University of Calgary.

NOTES

1 *Criticism and the Nineteenth Century* (London 1951) 7
2 In *Middlemarch: Critical Approaches to the Novel* (London 1967) 6-7
3 As in Quentin Anderson's important study of the novel, 'George Eliot in *Middlemarch,*' in *A Century of George Eliot Criticism* (London 1966) 313-24
4 Her term, in *Amos Barton,* chapter 5
5 'Idea and Image in the Novels of George Eliot,' in *Critical Essays on George Eliot* (London 1970) 166

THIS PARTICULAR WEB:
ESSAYS ON MIDDLEMARCH

BARBARA HARDY

Middlemarch and the passions

How shall we even begin to educate ourselves in the feelings?

Not by laying down laws or commandments, or axioms and postu-
lates. Not even by making assertions that such and such is blessed. Not
by words at all.

If we can't hear the cries far down in our own forests of dark veins,
we can look in the real novels, and there listen-in. Not listen to the
didactic statements of the author, but to the low, calling cries of the
characters, as they wander in the dark woods of their destiny.
(D.H. Lawrence, 'The Novel and the Feelings,' *Phoenix*)

The strange thing about life is that though the nature of it must have
been apparent to every one for hundreds of years, no one has left any
adequate account of it. The streets of London have their map; but our
passions are uncharted.
(Virginia Woolf, *Jacob's Room*)

In the 'Spanish Gypsy' there are seven arguments of about fifty pages
each. This is the way she describes passion.
(W.B. Yeats in a letter to F.J. Gregg, quoted in R. Ellmann, *The
Identity of Yeats*)

One of the less obvious sources of the greatness of *Middlemarch* is
its charting of the passions, in ways that sometimes come close to

Lawrence's recognition of the complexity and inarticulate eloquence of the life of feeling. Still, we cannot entirely ignore the author's didactic statements. Yeats was both right and wrong: *The Spanish Gypsy* does describe passion through argument, but George Eliot's novels are more responsive to the life of feeling than her poetry. Even in *Middlemarch* she uses statements about the passions as well as passionate enactment, needing words that classify psychological experience as well as words that stay faithfully and subtly close to the movement of feeling, in inner life and outer expression.

To begin with the didactic statement and argument. George Eliot usually introduces her major characters, not always right at the moment of dramatic entry, but fairly near it, in words that are clearly analytic, taxonomic, and instructive. Here are the discursive accompaniments to what is shown, as well as told, about Rosamond, Dorothea, and Lydgate.[1]

If you think it incredible that to imagine Lydgate as a man of family could cause thrills of satisfaction which had anything to do with the sense that she was in love with him, I will ask you to use your power of comparison a little more effectively, and consider whether red cloth or epaulets have never had an influence of that sort. *Our passions do not live apart in locked chambers*, but, dressed in their small wardrobe of notions, bring their provisions to a common table and mess together, feeding out of the common store according to their appetite. (16:123)

and

Into this soul-hunger as yet all her youthful *passion* was poured. (3:21)

and

All Dorothea's *passion* was transfused through a mind struggling towards an ideal life ... (5:32)

and

... that distinction of mind which belonged to his intellectual ardour, did not penetrate his feeling and judgment about furniture, or women,

or the desirability of its being know (without his telling) that he was
better born than other country surgeons. (15:111)

    In each analysis George Eliot attends to the place of the passions in
the psychic unity of character. She observes the difficulty caused by
the proximity of passions and by their separateness. Rosamond seems
to emerge as a case of insufficient discrimination, of a common but dan-
gerous 'messing together'; Dorothea too as a more intensely serious and
ardent case of similar merging; Lydgate as a counter-example of emotional segregation. All show a similar confidence and innocence about
their strong feelings, illustrating in their sharply individual ways D.H.
Lawrence's insistence on our brash creation of categories of feeling
which are not only inaccurate but lead to illusions of simplification and
control. 'We see love,' he observes in the essay already quoted, 'like a
woolly lamb or like a decorative, decadent panther in Paris clothes,
according as it is sacred or profane. We see hate, like a dog chained to a
kennel. We see fear, like a shivering monkey. We see anger, like a bull
with a ring through his nose, and greed like a pig.' George Eliot is not
dealing with such emblematic simplifications, but what she sees and
shows is very similar.

    The shift from the characters' inadequate knowledge to the author's
didactic analysis exposes the dangers of ignorant confidence. It is an
ignorance commonly encouraged by literature, like Casaubon's expectations about the nature of 'masculine passion,' which are pathetically
and abstractly grounded in his reading of the classics, and confounded
by the experience of his own disappointing ardours. He concludes that
'the poets had exaggerated the force of masculine passion;' but George
Eliot's parallels startle as often as they settle expectation, and just as
the altruistic Dorothea and the egocentric Rosamond are equally led
astray by the fatal association of feeling, so both the cold Casaubon
and the febrile Ladislaw are similarly misguided and let down by literary
expectation. The novel's discriminations are nice, and insist in many
ways that the names we commonly bestow on emotional experience
are inadequate: 'there are many wonderful mixtures in the world which
are all alike called love, and claim the privileges of a sublime rage.'

    The power of the passions in *Middlemarch* resides not only in the
telling but in the showing. The presentation of feeling is continuous,
running right through explicit commentary, behaviouristic description

of action, movement, gesture, and the drama of human relations and inner life. Each chapter has its trajectory of strong feelings. In chapter 42, for instance, George Eliot joins the emotional analysis of character with the inner drama of feeling. Both analysis and inner flow are marked by variety and motion. The conversation between doctor and patient, in which Lydgate tells Casaubon the diagnosis and prognosis, is marked by the mobile registrations of complex feeling. Lydgate feels 'a little amusement mingling with his pity' as he responds silently to Casaubon's pathetic and ridiculous speech about his life's 'possible importance,' but the author moves on to place this response through the irony of her foreknowledge: 'He was at present too ill acquainted with disaster to enter into the pathos of a lot where everything is below the level of tragedy except the passionate egoism of the sufferer.' This rash immature amusement is a silent one, and it is a sensitive sympathy which urges his question, ' "You refer to the possible hindrances from want of health?" he said, wishing to help forward Mr Casaubon's purpose, which seemed to be clogged by some hesitation.' Lydgate's controlled and measured sympathy is registered at the same time as Casaubon's clogging hesitation, doubt, fear, and anxiety. Perhaps the most poignant moment in this reticent passage is the comment that 'Mr Casaubon winced perceptibly, but bowed' as he begins to understand the drift of Lydgate's speech. When it is finished, the doctor's sympathy is registered once again, this time more purely, as an imaginative gesture of tact unmixed with amusement: 'Lydgate's instinct was fine enough to tell him that plain speech, quite free from ostentatious caution, would be felt by Mr Casaubon as a tribute of respect.' The emotional medium is full and fluent. Lydgate does not exactly feel respect, but feels the need to speak respectfully, and the nuance is movingly and candidly registered. What is not said is as important as what is said.

From this mute intercourse of feeling, we are drawn into Casaubon's solitude:

Lydgate, certain that his patient wished to be alone, soon left him; and the black figure with hands behind and head bent forward continued to pace the walk where the dark yew-trees gave him a mute companionship in melancholy, and the little shadows of bird or leaf that fleeted across the isles of sunlight, stole along in silence as in the presence of a sorrow. Here was a man who now for the first time found himself looking into the eyes of death — who was passing through one of those rare moments of experience when we feel the truth of a commonplace, which is as different from what we call knowing it, as the vision of waters upon the earth is different from the delirious vision of the water which cannot be had to cool the burning tongue. When the commonplace 'We must all die' transforms itself suddenly into the acute consciousness 'I must die — and soon,' then death grapples us, and his fingers are cruel; afterwards, he may come to fold us in his arms as our mother did, and our last moment of dim earthly discerning may be like the first. To Mr Casaubon now, it was as if he suddenly found himself on the dark river-bank and heard the plash of the oncoming oar, not discerning the forms, but expecting the summons. In such an hour the mind does not change its lifelong bias, but carries it onward in imagination to the other side of death, gazing backward — perhaps with the divine calm of beneficence, perhaps with the petty anxieties of self-assertion. What was Mr Casaubon's bias his acts will give us a clue to. He held himself to be, with some private scholarly reservations, a believing Christian, as to estimates of the present and hopes of the future. But what we strive to gratify, though we may call it a distant hope, is an immediate desire; the future estate for which men drudge up city alleys exists already in their imagination and love. And Mr Casaubon's immediate desire was not for divine communion and light divested of earthly conditions; his passionate longings, poor man, clung low and mist-like in very shady places.

This passage is startling in several ways. George Eliot is brilliantly, almost terrifyingly, imagining what can only be imagined, the moment of belief in one's own imminent death. Like her other moments of deep feeling, this combines something piercingly individual with an invocation of communal feeling, through the words 'We,' 'us,' and 'our mother,' through the common experience of childhood and death, memory and expectation, and through the solemn enlargement of the myth. Awe, loneliness, fear, passivity, are invoked through the culture and the myth, when George Eliot draws on Lethe, as Joyce was to do in his great summons of the myth of death in Paddy Dignam's funeral in *Ulysses*: 'the dark river-bank and ... the plash of the oncoming oar.'

But just as the resonance unnerves us, we leave it in a staggering return to particulars it cannot register. For the myth of Charon is invoked in order to be rejected. We rise to the awful occasion of death, but only for a moment. The sublime is deceptive, although it briefly permits pity and terror. Casaubon does not rise to the occasion. With the quiet and ironic comment on his beliefs, 'He held himself to be, with some private scholarly reservations, a believing Christian, as to estimates of the present and hopes of the future,' begins the return to what George Eliot calls elsewhere in the novel 'habitual self.' The beginning registers a scholarly Christian conformity which may temper the awfulness of Charon and Lethe. It is followed by a more devastating displacement of awe, fear, and suffering, in the return to Casaubon's jealous possessiveness. His passions as he faces Lethe are not those we have been led to imagine. Fear of death is weaker than fear of his widow's freedom, pity is just what his pride cannot accept, Lethe is just what his jealous egocentricity cannot entertain:

Consider that this was a mind which shrank from pity: have you ever watched in such a mind the effect of a suspicion that what is pressing it as a grief may be really a source of contentment, either actual or future, to the being who already offends by pitying?

Out of this analysis, necessarily conducted within and beyond the character's inner action, comes the well-known response to Dorothea's pity. She brings to Casaubon a sympathy that he cannot read, and as we move back from his solitude to the world of relationship, the conflict between his passions and Dorothea's takes its course. She makes her sensitive, loving movement of silence and contact; he keeps his hands rigid behind him so that her 'pliant arm' clings to his 'with difficulty.' So the chapter proceeds from the dumb show of hands and arms to Dorothea's solitude, where her anger and pity conflict in a morality play of passion invoking not a classical but a Christian myth. The drama shows Dorothea's capacity to check her feelings, and measures the distance she has travelled from that early time when her passions had been innocently in unison. What torments her is the knowledge that her best feelings cannot be communicated or received, that 'her best soul' is shut 'in prison.'

The last part of the chapter sets its scene in the familiar boudoir whose significant 'open bow-window' lets in 'the serene glory of the afternoon.' George Eliot uses the natural symbolism with apparent effortlessness, contrasting the serene glory with the unserene and inglorious human passions, while using the sunshine to register Dorothea's distressed carelessness of comfort: 'She threw herself on a chair, not heeding that she was in the dazzling sun-rays: if there were discomfort in that, how could she tell that it was not part of her inward misery?' The passions are recorded with due attention to the physical sensations. First is the generalized 'inward misery,' then 'the reaction of a rebellious anger stronger than any she had felt since her marriage. Instead of tears there came words: — "What have I done — what am I — that he should treat me so?" Hostile reproach is stopped by one of those moments of self-awareness recorded so steadily and imaginatively in Dorothea, 'She began to hear herself, and was checked into stillness.' The most amusingly and the most chillingly self-absorbed characters in the novels never hear themselves, and most of the sensitive souls don't manage it as often as Dorothea. Even with her, self-awareness doesn't come easily. It checks and silences, but silence is not followed by a quick recovery. Anger makes way for fatigue, bitterness, a jarringly lucid vision of her relation to her husband, contempt, and the beginning of rejection:

In the jar of her whole being, Pity was overthrown. Was it her fault that she had believed in him — had believed in his worthiness? — And what, exactly, was he? — She was able enough to estimate him — she who waited on his glances with trembling, and shut her best soul in prison, paying it only hidden visits, that she might be petty enough to please him. In such a crisis as this, some women begin to hate.

George Eliot's notation registers the motion and mixture of strong feeling through emotional personifications of a kind brilliantly but more commonly deployed by Fielding and Charlotte Brontë, and also through a vigorous *erlebte Rede* or free indirect style. The method is as mixed as the moods it records. George Eliot uses summary of feelings past and present, 'She had never deliberately allowed her resentment to govern her in this way before ...' She also provides generalization about the nature of the briefly ruling passion:

Her anger said, as anger is apt to say, that God was with her — that all heaven, though it were crowded with spirits watching them, must be on her side.

This splendid indictment of a self-righteousness clothed in spiritual garments is followed by action. Tantripp brings Casaubon's message that he wants to dine alone, which spikes the guns of Dorothea's anger; and, like Isabel Archer, she sits in a motionless, meditative struggle:

But the struggle changed continually, as that of a man who begins with a movement towards striking and ends with conquering his desire to strike. The energy that would animate a crime is not more than is wanted to inspire a resolved submission, when the noble habit of the soul reasserts itself. That thought with which Dorothea had gone out to meet her husband — her conviction that he had been asking about the possible arrest of all his work, and that the answer must have wrung his heart, could not be long without rising beside the image of him, like a shadowy monitor looking at her anger with sad remonstrance. It cost her a litany of pictured sorrows and of silent cries that she might be the mercy for those sorrows — but the resolved submission did come ...

Not only does she go out and wait for him, but he responds uncharacteristically with 'gentle surprise' and 'kind quiet melancholy.'

The characters relate to each other's emotions, and are changed by the relation. The particularity achieved has three aspects: truth to the moment, truth to the relationship, and truth to the human being.

A subtlety in *Middlemarch* is George Eliot's presentation of feeling as an influence upon conduct. If at times this presentation is intense and elevated, she concedes that such influence is often transitory. Casaubon is not, as Dorothea nobly but still erroneously imagines, solely occupied with fear and sorrow; he is planning the moves of his dead hand. Those gentle kind feelings are surprised out of him. They make no difference to what he chooses to do and be in the little life that remains. They are a tribute to Dorothea's moral seductiveness.

The crucial scene with Rosamond in chapter 81 is also marked by silent communication, touch, movement, and expression:

Looking like the lovely ghost of herself, her graceful slimness wrapped in her soft white shawl, the rounded infantine mouth and cheek inevitably suggesting mildness and innocence, Rosamond paused at three yards' distance from her visitor and bowed. But Dorothea, who had taken off her gloves, from an impulse which she could never resist when she wanted a sense of freedom, came forward, and with her face full of a sad yet sweet openness, put out her hand. Rosamond could not avoid meeting her glance, could not avoid putting her small hand into Dorothea's, which clasped it with gentle motherliness; and immediately a doubt of her own prepossessions began to stir within her. Rosamond's eye was quick for faces; she saw that Mrs Casaubon's face looked pale and changed since yesterday, yet gentle, and like the firm softness of her hand. But Dorothea had counted a little too much on her own strength: the clearness and intensity of her mental action this morning were the continuance of a nervous exaltation which made her frame as dangerously responsive as a bit of finest Venetian crystal; and in look-ing at Rosamond, she suddenly found her heart swelling, and was unable to speak — all her effort was required to keep back tears. She succeeded in that, and the emotion only passed over her face like the spirit of a sob; but it added to Rosamond's impression that Mrs Casaubon's state of mind must be something quite different from what she had imagined.

The cordial, pleading tones which seemed to flow with generous heedlessness above all the facts which had filled Rosamond's mind as grounds of obstruction and hatred between her and this woman, came as soothingly as a warm stream over her shrinking fears. Of course Mrs Casaubon had the facts in her mind, but she was not going to speak of anything connected with them. That relief was too great for Rosamond to feel much else at the moment.

Dorothea, completely swayed by the feeling that she was uttering, forgot everything but that she was speaking from out the heart of her own trial to Rosamond's. The emotion had wrought itself more and more into her utterance, till the tones might have gone to one's very marrow, like a low cry from some suffering creature in the darkness. And she had unconsciously laid her hand again on the little hand that she had pressed before.

Rosamond, with an overmastering pang, as if a wound within her had been probed, burst into hysterical crying as she had done the day before when she clung to her husband. Poor Dorothea was feeling a great wave of her own sorrow returning over her — her thought being drawn to the possible share that Will Ladislaw might have in Rosamond's mental tumult. She was beginning to fear that she should not be able to suppress herself enough to the end of this meeting, and while her hand was still resting on Rosamond's lap, though the hand underneath it was withdrawn, she was struggling against her own rising sobs. She tried to master herself with the thought that this might be a turning-point in three lives — not in her own; no, there the irrevocable had happened, but — in those three lives which were touching hers with the solemn neighbourhood of danger and distress. The fragile creature who was crying close to her — there might still be time to rescue her from the misery of false incompatible bonds; and this moment was unlike any other: she and Rosamond could never be together again with the same thrilling consciousness of yesterday within them both. She felt the relation between them to be peculiar enough to give her a peculiar influence, though she had no conception that the way in which her own feelings were involved was fully known to Mrs Lydgate.

When Rosamond's convulsed throat was subsiding into calm, and she withdrew the handkerchief with which she had been hiding her face, her eyes met Dorothea's as helplessly as if they had been blue flowers. What was the use of thinking about behaviour after this crying? And Dorothea looked almost as childish, with the neglected trace of a silent tear. Pride was broken down between these two.

The sense of physical strain and of mutual recognition is finely rendered. Even when the women talk, the words make less immediate impact than the tones of their voices. The imagery is excellently sensitive to the physical communication: 'as nervously responsive as a bit of finest Venetian crystal,' 'a warm stream,' 'one's very marrow,' 'As if a wound ... had been probed.' The continually changing struggle of anger and pity recorded and dramatised in the Casaubon scene was an inner action; this communication of nervous strain, good will, warmth, control, hysteria, and sorrow takes place in the public world, in a conventional drawing-room visit. It shows insight into the workings of dialogue without words as well as insight into the ways in which people feel together. Such mutual strong sympathy is usually preserved for scenes between lovers, in George Eliot as in other Victorian novelists, but this scene is exceptional in many ways. Dorothea's powers reach into the world of action, moving Rosamond to tell the truth about Will's feelings, but Rosamond goes back to her habitual self; the basil-plant survives. The particularity of this moment not only registers the strengths of emotional influence, but also contributes to a medium of feeling in which character is less stable and simple than Victorian fiction sometimes makes it out to be.

Even in the less powerful scenes of passionate crisis, feeling is related to thought and action. The characters think, act, and relate in a complex drama of feeling, the passions rise in intensity and crisis from the narrative flow. Even the minor characters draw much of their substance from such flow. But *Middlemarch* has one additional contribution to make to the story of human passion. Self-conscious in so many ways, tending like much great art to be about itself, to register its author's creative experiences, to assimilate forms and turn them into themes, it has something to divulge about the shaping power of feeling. Ladislaw's character is the nearest thing in the novel to a portrait of the artist, and a Romantic artist at that. Dorothea's elevated play of passion is not quite untouched by irony, and Will's is subjected to strong criticism. In chapter 47 the central character is Ladislaw, and the analysis of his love is instructive about feeling in the most dramatic fashion, since the lover learns through unlearning. What he unlearns is a simplification about the nature, place, and power of feeling.

Like Casaubon, Ladislaw has been educated in the passions by literature, not by the classical poets but the English:

What others might have called the futility of his passion, made an additional delight for his imagination: he was conscious of a generous movement, and of verifying in his own experience that higher love-poetry which had charmed his fancy. Dorothea, he said to himself, was for ever enthroned in his soul: no other woman could sit higher than her footstool; and if he could have written out in immortal syllables the effect she wrought within him, he might have boasted after the example of old Drayton, that —

'Queens hereafter might be glad to live
Upon the alms of her superfluous praise.'

This episode raises two interesting problems concerning strong feeling: how far can one choose feelings? and to what extent does a passionate imagination help the knowledge and control of feeling? The second question is the more personal. George Eliot seems to be interested in showing how a highly imaginative and sensitive mind can be as wrong about anticipation and control as that of an ardent girl or a too inhibited pedant. I am not sure if she has mastered the problem she has set in this chapter, and it might be argued that the dramatic action carries more truth than the generalization and analysis. It is perhaps an episode which grows in subtlety in the writing. Certainly, the chapter's motto seems more confined in simplicities than what follows:

Was never true love loved in vain,
For truest love is highest gain.
No art can make it: it must spring
Where elements are fostering.
So in heaven's spot and hour
Springs the little native flower,
Downward root and upward eye,
Shapen by the earth and sky.

The motto applies in a general way to the story of Will and Dorothea, but is much more simple than the prose action.

Will is presented in a characteristic emotional complexity: he is, as usual, adoring, and, as often, irritable. His emotions are linked with the 'heat,' irritability, and restlessness of his response to Lydgate in the preceding chapter. George Eliot shows the mixture finely, since the restless feelings continue in a desire to see Dorothea and find another vent in plaguing Casaubon; the irritation with Lydgate hooks on to Casaubon as a more appropriate object, and his adoration carries on, steady, but

sealed-off from the world of action. Will's love has a certain strength
and a certain weakness in being insulated from the possibilities of
ordinary love:

Was he not making a fool of himself? — and at a time when he was more
than ever conscious of being something better than a fool? And for
what end?

Well, for no definite end. True, he had dreamy visions of possibilities: there is no human being who having both passions and thoughts
does not think in consequence of his passions — does not find images
rising in his mind which soothe the passion with hope or sting it with
dread. But this, which happens to us all, happens to some with a wide
difference; and Will was not one of those whose wit 'keeps the road-
way:' he had his bypaths where there were little joys of his own choosing, such as gentlemen cantering on the highroad might have thought
rather idiotic. The way in which he made a sort of happiness for himself out of his feeling for Dorothea was an example of this. It may seem
strange, but it is the fact, that the ordinary vulgar vision of which Mr
Casaubon suspected him — namely, that Dorothea might become a
widow, and that the interest he had established in her mind might turn
into acceptance of him as a husband — had no tempting, arresting
power over him; he did not live in the scenery of such an event, and
follow it out, as we all do with that imagined 'otherwise' which is our
practical heaven. It was not only that he was unwilling to entertain
thoughts which could be accused of baseness, and was already uneasy
in the sense that he had to justify himself from the charge of ingrati-
tude — the latent consciousness of many other barriers between himself
and Dorothea besides the existence of her husband, had helped to turn
away his imagination from speculating on what might befall Mr Casaubon. And there were yet other reasons. Will, we know, could not bear
the thought of any flaw appearing in his crystal: he was at once exas-
perated and delighted by the calm freedom with which Dorothea
looked at him and spoke to him, and there was something so exquisite
in thinking of her just as she was, that he could not long for a change
which must somehow change her. Do we not shun the street version of
a fine melody? — or shrink from the news that the rarity — some bit of
chiselling or engraving perhaps — which we have dwelt on even with

exultation in the trouble it has cost us to snatch glimpses of it, is really not an uncommon thing, and may be obtained as an everyday possession?

George Eliot's benevolence does not prevent her being cunning. She permits the recognition that passions shape images, and a gentle irony, easy to miss, explains how Will makes 'joys of his own choosing.' A luxury of passion, this choosing of joy. George Eliot herself seems to waver rather uncertainly between an approval of Will's freedom from 'the ordinary vulgar vision ... that Dorothea might become a widow' and a recognition of the limits of adoration. She seems to have a real feeling for Will's sense that his adoration is rare and remote, endorsing his chivalric worshipping in the image of the street version of a fine melody. But more critically ironic is the comparison of his identification to the 'rarity — some bit of chiselling or engraving perhaps — which we have dwelt on with exultation in the trouble it has cost us to snatch glimpses of it' which we suddenly learn, shrinking, 'may be obtained as an every-day possession.' Both similes are followed by a statement of apparent approval: 'Our good depends on the quality and breadth of our emo-tion.' This didactic statement of value, made through the imagery of measurement, may make us feel uncertain, less because of the associa-tions of the words than because of the claim made: is it in fact so easy to measure such quality and such breadth? George Eliot is a great an-alyst of the passions, but it would be foolish to claim that the analysis never falters into facility. Will is to obtain his love 'as an everyday possession'; worship, adoration, higher love-poetry, queens, and foot-stools are inappropriate images for love in the quotidian world of *Mid-dlemarch*. In a way, George Eliot seems to know this, or at least to glimpse the deficiency of those troubadour images.

The chapter moves from Will's love — half-endorsed, half-criticized — to his enjoyment of jealousy and malice, in a morality play of Petty Objection and Sublime Inclination. The conquest of conscience cheers him up and makes him complacent, and George Eliot registers a rare pas-sage of content, purchased, like much content, by fantasy rather than rational anticipation. It is a spiteful as well as a sweet intent; Will feels joyful not just because he is journeying sunnily towards his love, 'skirt-ing the wood, where the sunlight fell broadly under the budding

boughs ... Everything seemed to know it was Sunday, and to approve of
his going to Lowick Church,' but also because he is amused at the
thought of annoying Casaubon. The spring idyll is not idyllically
grounded in noble feeling.

Out of the day, the expectation, and the content, comes the one
lyric of the novel, a fragile flight of feeling caught in the great prose
narrative:

> O me, O me, what frugal cheer
> > My love doth feed upon!
> A touch, a ray, that is not here,
> > A shadow that is gone:
>
> A dream of breath that might be near,
> > An inly-echoed tone,
> The thought that one may think me dear,
> > The place where one was known,
>
> The tremor of a banished fear,
> > An ill that was not done —
> O me, O me, what frugal cheer
> > My love doth feed upon!

The lyric is the one proof of Will's creative powers and by no means
a bad one. But its merits are less important than its function. It is immediately followed by the appropriate description of the 'delicate throat'
of the singer, and of his springlike brilliance; 'he looked like an incarnation of the spring whose spirit filled the air – a bright creature, abundant
in uncertain promises.' The hinge on which this chapter of the passions
turns is the 'uncertain promise.' Will is residing in his passionate moment, framing and forming it through lyric, and George Eliot seems to
question and define the nature of his poetic medium by placing it in
the testing flow of narrative action.

She first contrasts its purity of feeling with the impure source in life.
Lyric derives its power from isolating strong feeling, and the novelist
provides the history from which lyric is usually happily cut off. The
poem which is 'not exactly a hymn' but which fits Will's 'Sunday

experience,' does so only by ignoring jealousy and malice and concentrating on longing and love. Will is no unimaginative selector from emotional experience, and has not lightly been compared with Shelley or allowed wisdom on the subject of poetry. In chapter 22 he tells Dorothea: 'To be a poet is to have a soul so quick to discern, that no shade of quality escapes it, and so quick to feel, that discernment is but a hand playing with finely-ordered variety on the chords of emotion.' In that same chapter George Eliot qualifies her comments on Will's habits of amorous worship, remarking that while 'remote worship of a woman throned' plays an important part in men's lives, the 'worshipper longs for some queenly recognition,' and she probably expects the reader to carry in his mind some recollection of the things she said and showed in Will's contradictory 'imaginative demands' in those scenes in Rome. The contrast in this later episode between lyric purity and the impure source still permits the poem to possess 'finely-ordered variety.' Will's hymn-like lyric admits the undernourished state of remote worship; does sweetly if faintly lament frugality in 'O me, O me'; does show the delicious items in love's diet — 'a touch, a ray, a shadow, a dream of breath, a tone, a thought, a place,' and the unpalatable ones — a tremor of fear, 'An ill that was not done.' This courtly worship is trying to imagine starvation as well as nourishment. But when the imagined future comes, it confounds the lyric poet.

For the lyric of love is not only given a past, which throws its purity into special relief; it is also given a future. Will gets that taste of frugal cheer which he has so sweetly sighed over in his poem, but its taste is simply sour. The sympathetic weather, the dream, tone, place of the lyric longing, all turn out to have held uncertain promises. The promises are broken as soon as Will arrives at Lowick church. All his expectations go awry. He has expected to sit with the curate's family, but the Tuckers have left Lowick; he has expected to enjoy the sight of Dorothea, but finds that he dares not look at her; he is surprised by discomfort, realizes that she may be upset, that he may have blundered, and that the expected amusement at Casaubon's expense is not forthcoming: 'It was no longer amusing to vex Mr Casaubon, who had the advantage probably of watching him and seeing that he dared not turn his head. Why had he not imagined this beforehand?'

Will's actual feelings make plain the simplifications of lyric purity, as the poet moves from the delightful indulgences of image-worship to the destructive extreme of self-contempt, hostility, and cynicism:

There was no delivering himself from his cage, however; and Will found his places and looked at his book as if he had been a school mistress; feeling that the morning service had never been so immeasurably long before, that he was utterly ridiculous, out of temper, and miserable. This was what a man got by worshipping the sight of a woman!

In a novel which at least tries to deal plainly with unideal existence, this rejection of worship is an important strand in the pattern of feeling. It would be hard to argue, however, that George Eliot is thoroughly clear and full in analyzing the descent of Will and Dorothea into the ordinary world. It is a descent implied in the Finale[2] of the novel, and touched on in this episode; but in the later passages describing their farewell and final union George Eliot still surrounds the lovers with a dazzling halo. There is no dazzle here. Will Ladislaw leaves Lowick, having to 'walk back sadly at mid-day along the same road which he had trodden hopefully in the morning. The lights were all changed for him both without and within.' He writes no more poems, and perhaps the reader knows why.

A novelist who also writes poetry is in a good position to appraise the dangers of lyric. Lyric isolates the moment of passion, cuts off the historical flow backwards and onwards in time, and thus enacts the timeless ritual of passion itself. There are lyrics (Donne's or Shakespeare's) that manage to convey both the intensity and the sense of its mortal bonds. *Middlemarch* conveys the intensity, but keeps it in time and place.

The Sunday morning itself confounds Will's idyllic and selective expectations about Sunday mornings, dreams as idyllic and selective as those in the poem, though rendered in prose — 'I have always liked the quaintness of the church and congregation; besides, I know the Tuckers: I shall go into their pew.' George Eliot said early in the chapter that our anticipations are shaped by passion, that we 'find images' which 'soothe the passion with hope or sting it with dread,' and she shows Will making his desirable, sympathetic, and selective background image of society and environment. Church, congregation, and curate all fall into place in his imaginary forecast; the church and congregation 'idyllic,' the curate conveniently where he used to be. It turns out, however, that the congregation of Lowick is less pastorally stable than Will's image has expected: the Tuckers have moved on, instead of staying in their pew as handy minor characters, and there is a new face, 'Mr Rigg's frog-face ... something alien and unaccountable.' 'The place where one was known' has not stood still. The 'group of rural faces' has changed slightly, and George Eliot insists on this change through Will's discomfited expectations, and through another spring image, tough in its implications, 'hardly with more change than we see in the boughs of a tree which breaks here and there with age, but yet has young shoots.' We are always aware of the passage of time in *Middlemarch*.

Things have changed, people have slightly shifted position even in Lowick 'at peace' in 1831, 'not more agitated by Reform than by the solemn tenor of the Sunday sermon.' But George Eliot is not just registering history as 'background.' Society's slow change mirrors Will's anachronistic and literary habits of worship. It is out of the feudal sense of place and hierarchy that 'the three generations of decent cottagers came ... with a sense of duty to their betters generally − the smaller children regarding Mr Casaubon, who wore the black gown and mounted to the highest box, as probably the chief of all betters, and the one most awful if offended.' The implications of this comic version of deference are various: Casaubon is powerful and is offended, and nearly keeps Dorothea and Will apart for good. More important in the union of social chronicle and drama of passion is George Eliot's display of the community of socially determined attitudes and feelings, where they emerge in deference to squire, vicar, or throned queen. The feminist impatience, which runs through the novel, pervades the analysis of adoration, but it is enlarged to take in other versions of misplaced deference.

Will's lyric is not only unaware of the social links between its passionate moment and lower forms or lesser variants, it is also unaware of the thickly peopled world. In this inveterately social novel, we are perpetually reminded of the community. George Eliot insists[3] on placing her drama of personal passion in the peopled environment. The 'quaint' congregation has its point of view, too. It is composed of people who also tend, like Will, to look up, and who are also all making up their experience with self-flattering bias and selection. A comic displacement urges this multiple viewpoint as a social and psychological truth, amusing but serious:

> The congregation had been used to seeing Will at church in former days, and no one took much note of him except the quire, who expected him to make a figure in the singing.

> The clerk observed with surprise that Mr Ladislaw did not join in the tune of Hanover, and reflected that he might have a cold.

The clerk and members of the congregation are not rustic fools designed to frame fine intensities, but human reminders that passion occurs, as Auden says, 'While someone else is eating or opening a window or just walking dully along.' It is probably more precise and more faithfully attentive to the art of George Eliot to say that one passion is seen to occur in the world of everyone else's passion. To the choir and the clerk, Will is someone who will figure in the music. If he is silent, it is because he must have a cold. Such density and candour go to make the richness and reality of *Middlemarch*, registering the problems of passion in that world of ordinary experience which was George Eliot's province.

NOTES

1 The italics in the immediately following passages are mine. George Eliot uses the term 'passions' as freely as Fielding.
2 'Dorothea herself had no dreams of being praised above other ... women' and 'Certainly those determining acts of her life were not ideally beautiful.'
3 As Dickens did too, for instance, in the brilliant psychological analysis of the professional and social shaping of Bradley Headstone in *Our Mutual Friend*.

GORDON S. HAIGHT

George Eliot's 'eminent failure,' Will Ladislaw

In 1886 James Knowles, the editor of the *Nineteenth Century*, gave a
dinner party which included the Prime Minister Mr Gladstone, the
French Ambassador Monsieur Waddington, and the American Minister
Mr Edward Phelps. During the evening when conversation turned towards the English novel, Knowles declared that George Eliot's *Middlemarch* 'would live long beyond any other – including [those of] Scott
– he did not care for Scott. Gladstone upheld Scott – and *Middlemarch* too,' though he felt the unsatisfactory nature of all the marriages
in George Eliot's novels as compared with Scott's, which he remembered
reading as a boy, lying on his stomach in the grass, 'as they came out in
numbers.'[1] But the two foreign diplomats agreed that in France and in
America '*Middlemarch* was scarcely known, while every one read
Scott.' Monsieur Waddington was probably right about France; but Mr
Phelps must have been speaking only for the older generation. Yale had
just graduated Wilbur Cross, who was already beginning his work on
The Development of the English Novel (1899), in which he declares
that 'George Eliot gave prose fiction a substance which it had never before had among any people' (p 150). In my own undergraduate days she
was still being read, and I am inclined to believe the notion that her
books ever lay on the shelves unopened is a vulgar error.

Few novels have borne such intensive critical scrutiny. Before his un-
timely death W.J. Harvey gave us admirable accounts of the contemporary reviews and of the special studies which proliferated so rapidly

after 1940. One of the essays in Barbara Hardy's *Middlemarch: Critical Approaches to the Novel* (1967), J.M.S. Tompkins' brilliant 'Plea for Ancient Lights,' outlined the trend of criticism in the years since it came to be treated as a 'Sacred Book.'

If the literal and even the historical meanings of the text appeared re- mote and irrelevant, the allegorical and the anagogical could be tried. In something the same way, story, character and setting — those prime data of the nineteenth-century novel — can be pushed aside with slight and sometimes imperfect inspection, while the keen analytic intellects of the modern critical scene apply themselves to elucidate the formal relations, the ideal structures, the metaphors, overt and submerged, and the key-words and phrases of the work in hand. Sometimes we are car- ried beyond the identification of conscious artistry and invited to dis- cern, in sequences and recurrences of allied terms, the movements of the novelist's unconscious mind. Some of these words are no more than parts of the machinery of the language, reduced metaphors and dead symbols found in everyday talk, unrealized images with no salient mean- ing. But 'crumble' the text sufficiently, and there they are, and we may suppose that the unconscious is expressed through this subtle and archaic means; and since what is left of the doctrine of inspiration is now related to the activity of the unconscious, we may do well to study it *in minimis*, as early commentators studied the syllables of what they took to be the Holy Spirit. (p 172)

Miss Tompkins' worst example of this 'shredded and crumbled' text was Mark Schorer's unhappy discovery of a 'nearly systematic Christ anal- ogy' in Will Ladislaw, which she deftly disposed of. Her lucid summary of Will's contradictory qualities gives a more sympathetic view of the young man than most critics have bestowed on him. Henry James, for instance, wrote in 1873.

The figure of Will Ladislaw is a beautiful attempt, with many finely- completed points; but on the whole it seems to us a failure. It is the only eminent failure in the book, and its defects are therefore the more striking. It lacks sharpness of outline and depth of color; we have not found ourselves believing in Ladislaw as we believe in Dorothea, in

Mary Garth, in Rosamond, in Lydgate, in Mr Brooke and Mr Casaubon. He is meant, indeed, to be a light creature (with a large capacity for gravity, for he finally gets into Parliament), and a light creature certainly should not be heavily drawn. The author, who is evidently very fond of him, has found for him here and there some charming and eloquent touches; but in spite of these he remains vague and impalpable to the end.[2]

Virginia Woolf, writing in the *Times Literary Supplement* in 1919, just two days before the centenary of George Eliot's birth, regretted that Dorothea could not have been provided with a better mate than Will Ladislaw; Oliver Elton called him 'mere pasteboard'; to Lord David Cecil he was 'a schoolgirl's dream, and a vulgar dream at that.' F.R. Leavis in his uncompromising style dismissed him completely:

In fact, he has no independent status of his own — he can't be said to exist; he merely represents, not a dramatically real point of view, but certain of George Eliot's intentions — intentions she has failed to realize creatively. The most important of these is to impose on the reader her own vision and valuation of Dorothea.

Will, of course, is also intended — it is not really a separate matter — to be, in contrast to Casaubon, a fitting soul-mate for Dorothea. He is not substantially (everyone agrees) 'there' ...[3]

Almost every one, perhaps. I have recorded elsewhere my dissent from Dr Leavis' concept of Dorothea as the 'product of George Eliot's own 'soul-hunger' — another day-dream ideal self.'[4] Now his contemptuous dismissal of Ladislaw prompts me to look again at that much abused young man.

If Ladislaw is to be regarded as unrealized or non-existent, it cannot be on grounds of his appearance. George Eliot describes him indirectly, dropping details here and there and avoiding the formal introductory accounts we are used to in Scott and Trollope.[5] He is tall and slim — Miss Noble hardly comes up to his elbow, Dorothea only to his shoulder — and moves with the quickness suggested by the word 'mercurial.' In a distinctive way he is handsome. At first sight Celia, who is conspicuously sensitive to people's faces, pronounces him 'quite nice-looking.' Even the aristocratic Mrs Cadwallader twice calls him 'a pretty sprig ... He is like the fine old Crichley portraits before the idiots came in.' He has 'grey eyes, rather near together, a delicate irregular nose with a little ripple in it,' a prominent chin and jaw, and a throat and neck reminiscent of the Romantic poets. When he was first presented to Mr Casaubon's young fiancée, his expression had rather a pouting air of discontent, though a few moments later, when he was alone, his 'sense of the ludicrous lit up his features very agreeably.' A 'merry' smile was his usual expression, a 'sunny' smile like 'a gush of inward light illuminating the transparent skin as well as the eyes, and playing about every curve and line.' He had a light complexion — a girl's complexion' it is called once — that made his face and throat flush suddenly under the stress of strong feeling. His light brown hair was 'not immoderately long' — at least compared with his German artist friends' at Rome — but 'abundant and curly' and seemed to shake out light when he turned his head quickly and, with his most characteristic gesture, threw his head back.

Some of these traits annoy readers, especially those hunting for reasons to justify their dislike of Ladislaw. The way young men wear their hair has been a divisive factor at least since the days of Cavalier and Roundhead. When Lewes' son was about to leave school in Switzerland, his father warned him not to have his hair cut short as schoolboys then did. 'Let it grow nice and long,' he wrote, 'so that when your mother embraces you she may embrace a good-looking chap.'[6] Today both Ladislaw's curls and his habit of stretching himself at full length on the rug are accepted more sympathetically by the young, with whom his contempt for stuffy convention ranks him as modern. They can understand, too, his experiments with fasting and with drugs, which he had tried thoroughly enough to convince him that there was an entire dissimilarity between his constitution and De Quincey's. His dress was not freakish, but there was something a little foreign-looking about him. He had lived abroad almost as long as in England: after five or six years at Rugby (before Dr Arnold's time) he declined to go up to Oxford or Cambridge, but went instead to study at Heidelberg. Though proud of his honour as a gentleman, he was quite indifferent to class. In Rome

... he was given to ramble about among the poor people, and the taste did not quit him in Middlemarch.

He had somehow picked up a troop of droll children, little hatless boys with their galligaskins much worn and scant shirting to hang out, little girls who tossed their hair out of their eyes to look at him, and guardian brothers at the mature age of seven. This troop he had led out on gypsy excursions to Halsell Wood at nutting-time, and once the cold weather had set in he had taken them on a clear day to gather sticks for a bonfire in the hollow of a hillside, where he drew out a small feast of gingerbread for them, and improvised a Punch-and-Judy drama with some private home-made puppets. (46:339).

There was something of the gypsy in him, a rebellious spirit that hated conventional restrictions. However one feels about this character, it is absurd to pronounce it vague or impalpable.

The objection most often made is that Ladislaw is a dilettante. He does not contradict his friend Naumann's accusation that he is amateurish as a painter, but insists that 'daubing a little' has taught him something about art that he could not have learned without it. A career in painting would be 'too one-sided a life' for him. Even with years of drudgery he could never hope to do well what had already been done better by others. This is clearly an oblique judgment on the futile labour of Mr Casaubon, who attributed Will's aversion to adopting a profession to dislike of steady application — a virtue which had yet to produce the first chapter of the Key to All Mythologies. Will's brief engagement as assistant in that mighty work was terminated, not by his lack of thoroughness, but by Mr Casaubon's morbid fear of being judged, which was soon to dismay Dorothea. Will's glib remark that 'If Mr Casaubon read German he would save himself a great deal of trouble' was a highly superficial criticism. The two most important books by Germans were already available to him: Creuzer's *Mythologie* (1810-12) had appeared in a French translation, and Lobeck's *Aglaophamus* (1829) was written in Latin. George Eliot comments: 'Young Mr Ladislaw was not at all deep himself in German writers; but very little achievement is required in order to pity another man's shortcomings.' Since leaving Lowick, Will had spent his time in Germany and Italy, 'sketching plans for several dramas, trying prose and finding it too jejune, trying verse and finding it too artificial, beginning to copy "bits" from old pictures, leaving off because they were "no good," and observing that, after all, self-culture was the principal point.' His apparently aimless wandering among artists and writers, among the students at Heidelberg and the poor people of Rome, had taught him a good deal about life. He is ready to give up his dependence on the allowance from Mr Casaubon and return to England to work his own way. He accepts Mr Brooke's offer to edit the *Pioneer* as much to be near Dorothea as to be independent of her husband, who banishes him from Lowick more out of jealousy than because the career of journalist was unsuited to his rank as a second cousin, or, more accurately, a first cousin once removed.

'The impression once given that [Ladislaw] is a *dilettante*,' Henry James wrote, 'is never properly removed.' Careful reading, I think, reveals a slight change in Will's attitude. At Rome he had told Dorothea:

The best piety is to enjoy — when you can. You are doing the most then to save the earth's character as an agreeable planet. And enjoyment radiates. It is of no use to try and take care of all the world; that is being taken care of when you feel delight — in art or in anything else. Would you turn all the youth of the world into a tragic chorus, wailing and moralising over misery? I suspect that you have some false belief in the virtues of misery, and want to make your life a martyrdom. (22:163).

This philosophy seems to make Will a forerunner of Pater's New Hedonism, which has been examined so suggestively in U.C. Knoepflmacher's *Religious Humanism and the Victorian Novel* (1965). Later, however, at Tipton Grange, though still rebellious against submitting to anything he dislikes, Will professes 'To love what is good and beautiful when I see it' (39:287). Here the element of the 'good' sounds a new note, and his love for Dorothea directs his interest more and more to the practical reforms she is concerned with. He plans to study law to prepare himself for public service, a phase of his career that some may feel to have been inadequately realized. Like Lydgate's successful medical practice in the fashionable Continental bathing-place, it occurs off-stage at the end of the novel, when the multifarious threads must be quickly drawn together. Though it is only briefly mentioned, it is none the less genuine.

Some contemporary reviewers looked askance at Ladislaw's morals, concurring in Sir James' opinion of him as 'a man of little principle and light character' (84:597). Their most serious charge was 'his unworthy flirtation with his friend Lydgate's wife.'[8] Only a censorious and evil-minded moralist would object if an attractive bachelor of twenty-five, unjustly excluded from the society in which he properly belongs, enjoys singing and chatting with the 'prettiest girl in Middlemarch.' Lydgate himself, with no ear whatever for music, had succumbed to Rosamond's other charms. He shows no sign of jealousy, nor is there the least impropriety in Will's conduct. Twice the Quarry states plainly (pp 11, 26) that it is 'Rosamond's flirtation with Ladislaw,' not his with Rosamond, and George Eliot's careful exploration of her fantasy makes the fact quite clear. Will returned to Middlemarch, not to see Rosamond, but in hope of some accident by which he might meet Dorothea. Ironically, he does. At the very instant Dorothea surprises them, Will is telling Rosamond that he loves another, that he can never love her. Even Dr Leavis concedes – in a footnote – that Ladislaw is 'adequate' in this cruel disillusioning of Rosamond.

But he takes particular exception to the 'presentment of those impossibly high-falutin' *tête-à-tête* – or soul to soul –exchanges between Dorothea and Will, which is utterly without irony or criticism.'[9] Now, with all due reverence for irony, which has, perhaps, had more than its share, I think we may ask whether it has much to contribute to a love scene. Shakespeare certainly eschews it in his 'presentment' of the 'exchanges' between Romeo and Juliet. But it is simply untrue that Ladislaw's interviews with Dorothea are ever without irony or criticism. In chapter 54, their first meeting after Casaubon's death, Dorothea assumes that Will knows about the disgusting codicil, and from his announcement that he is leaving Middlemarch concludes that he had never felt more than friendship for her. The reader knows that she is wrong on both counts. When she says that she will be glad to hear he has made his value felt, but that he must be patient, for it may be a long while, Will could hardly save himself from falling down at her feet. George Eliot here interjects: 'He used to say that the horrible hue and surface of

crape dress was most likely the sufficient controlling force. This little
touch of distancing humour Dr Leavis ignores. Again, though Will has
come bitterly resolved that their meeting should not end with 'a confes-
sion which might be interpreted into asking for her fortune,' Dorothea
is all the while preoccupied with the hardship of his probable want of
money, 'while she had what ought to have been his share' and was pre-
vented from giving it to him. All she can ask is whether he would like
the miniature of his grandmother, which Will irritably refuses: 'It would
be more consoling if others wanted to have it ... Why should I have
that, when I have nothing else? A man with only a portmanteau for his
stowage must keep his memorials in his head.' Though he was 'merely
venting his petulance,' for Dorothea 'his words had a peculiar sting,'
and she replied: 'You are much the happier of us two, Mr Ladislaw, to
have nothing.' But Will, without the least thought of any claim on
Casaubon's property, only says that he regrets poverty because 'it divides us from what we most care for.' The whole scene is suffused with
irony, which culminates in the appearance of Sir James Chettam. His
mingled feelings, too, are subtly analyzed. Though he had assumed that
they were lovers, by entering at just that moment Sir James incorpo-
rates 'the strongest reasons through which Will's pride became a repel-
lent force, keeping him asunder from Dorothea.' To see no irony here is
sheer perversity.

Nearly two months pass before their next interview (chapter 62).
Then Will, having learned from Rosamond about the codicil and from
Raffles about the scandal involving his mother's family, wrote to
Dorothea, asking permission to call again at Lowick. He

felt the awkwardness of asking for more last words. His former farewell
had been made in the hearing of Sir James Chettam, and had been announced as final even to the butler. It is certainly trying to a man's dignity to reappear when he is not expected to do so: a first farewell has
pathos in it, but to come back for a second lends an opening to comedy,
and it was possible even that there might be bitter sneers afloat about
Will's motives for lingering. Still it was on the whole more satisfactory
to his feeling to take the directest means of seeing Dorothea, than to use
any device which might give an air of chance to a meeting of which he
wished her to understand that it was what he earnestly sought. (62:458)

Ironically, Dorothea did not receive his note, but met him quite by
chance at the Grange, where Will had come to fetch the portfolio of
his sketches; at the moment she entered the library he was thinking
hopefully that he might find an answer from her awaiting him at Middlemarch and was smiling at the sketch which on the first day he ever
saw her had 'a relation to nature too mysterious for Dorothea' (62:461).
She had just come from Freshitt Hall with her feelings exacerbated by
Mrs Cadwallader's malicious gossip (inspired by Sir James) about 'Orlan-
do' Ladislaw's always being found lying on the rug at Lydgate's house
or warbling with his wife. Though she had repudiated the report indig-
nantly, Dorothea could not forget that the only time she went to the
house she had found Ladislaw there and heard him singing. Feeling 'a
strange alternation between anger with Will and the passionate defence
of him,' Dorothea arrived at the Grange.

Will, too, was in an angry mood. The hateful codicil had completely
shattered his dream of being able to return some day to ask Dorothea
to marry him, and he could not conceal his irritation:

'I have been grossly insulted in your eyes and in the eyes of others.
There has been a mean implication against my character. I wish you to
know that under no circumstances would I have lowered myself by —
under no circumstances would I have given men the chance of saying
that I sought money under the pretext of seeking — something else.
There was no need of other safeguard against me — the safeguard of
wealth was enough.'

Throughout this brief scene their feelings are always at cross purposes,
preventing their saying directly what they mean.

'What I care more for than I can ever care for anything else is absolutely forbidden to me — I don't mean merely by being out of my reach,
but forbidden me, even if it were within my reach, by my own pride
and honour — by everything I respect myself for. Of course I shall go on
living as a man might do who had seen heaven in a trance.'

Will paused, imagining that it would be impossible for Dorothea to
misunderstand this; indeed he felt that he was contradicting himself
and offending against his self-approval in speaking to her so plainly;

but still — it could not be fairly called wooing a woman to tell her that he would never woo her. It must be admitted to be a ghostly kind of wooing.

But Dorothea's mind was rapidly going over the past with quite another vision than his. The thought that she herself might be what Will most cared for did throb through her an instant, but then came doubt; the memory of the little they had lived through together turned pale and shrank before the memory which suggested how much fuller might have been the intercourse between Will and some one else with whom he had had constant companionship. Everything he had said might refer to that other relation, and whatever had passed between him and herself was thoroughly explained by what she had always regarded as their simple friendship and the cruel obstruction thrust upon it by her husband's injurious act. Dorothea stood silent, with her eyes cast down dreamily, while images crowded upon her which left the sickening certainty that Will was referring to Mrs Lydgate. But why sickening? He wanted her to know that here too his conduct should be above suspicion. (62:463-4)

Will's mind was also 'tumultuously busy while he watched her,' and he 'could not deny that a secret longing for the assurance that she loved him was at the root of all his words.' They both stood silent until the footman announced that her carriage was ready. Her parting words 'seemed to him cruelly cold and unlike herself.'

'I have never done you injustice. Please remember me,' said Dorothea, repressing a rising sob.

'Why should you say that?' said Will, with irritation. 'As if I were not in danger of forgetting everything else.'

He had really a movement of anger against her at that moment, and it impelled him to go away without pause. It was all one flash to Dorothea — his last words — his distant bow to her as he reached the door — the sense that he was no longer there. (62:464)

The *erlebte Rede* describing her mingled joy at realizing that Will loved her and her sorrow for the irrevocable parting is richly imagined. A few minutes later, when she overtook him on the road, she longed to but could not make some sign that would seem to say 'Need we part?' She wished that she could give him the money to make things easier for him. But Will saw Dorothea driving past him as he plodded along with an increased bitterness that made his rudeness to her seem a matter of necessity. How can one read this brief, restrained episode as if George Eliot were seeing Dorothea through Will's eyes and utterly without irony?

I find nothing in the diction of these scenes to deserve Dr Leavis' quaint 'highfalutin.' Without bothering to discuss the interviews he declares:

Their tone and quality is given fairly enough in this retrospective summary (it occurs at the end of Chapter LXXXII): 'all their vision, all their thought of each other, had been in a world apart, where the sunshine fell on tall white lilies, where no evil lurked, and no other soul entered'. It is Will who is supposed to be reflecting to this effect, but Will here − as everywhere in his attitude towards Dorothea − is unmistakably not to be distinguished from the novelist (as we have noted, he hardly exists).[10]

On reconsideration Dr Leavis might soften this opinion: read in its entirety I do not think the passage in chapter 82 can support his view that Will's valuation of Dorothea is George Eliot's. It comes immediately after Rosamond says that she has told Mrs Casaubon the truth about her relations with him.

The effect of these words was not quite all gladness. As Will dwelt on them with excited imagination, he felt his cheeks and ears burning at the thought of what had occurred between Dorothea and Rosamond − at the uncertainty how far Dorothea might still feel her dignity wounded in having an explanation of his conduct offered to her. There might still remain in her mind a changed association with him which made an irremediable difference −a lasting flaw. With active fancy he wrought himself into a state of doubt little more easy than that of the man who has escaped from wreck by night and stands on unknown ground in the darkness. Until that wretched yesterday − except the moment of vexation long ago in the very same room and in the very same

presence — all their vision, all their thought of each other, had been as
in a world apart, where the sunshine fell on tall white lilies, where no
evil lurked, and no other soul entered. But now — would Dorothea
meet him in that world again? (82:589)

Ben Jonson dared ask, 'Have you seen but a white lily grow / Before
rude hands have touch'd it?' and for earlier and later poets the lily has
symbolized an ideal love. In 1870 to readers familiar with Pre-Raphaelite poems and paintings it would have seemed entirely natureal for a
poetic young lover to express his feelings 'as in a world apart, where
the sunshine fell on tall white lilies.'
    Chapter 83 follows immediately with its epigraph from Donne,

And now good-morrow to our waking souls
Which watch not one another out of fear;
For love all love of other sights controls,
And makes one little room, an everywhere,

an appropriate motto for the chapter ending with Dorothea's eager em-
bracing of poverty. One might fear that this ultimate 'soul to soul ex-
change' would prove the most 'highfalutin' of all. But it does not. Dorothea's short, simple, direct sentences belie the emotion underlying
them. Derek Oldfield's splendid essay on 'The Character of Dorothea'
(in *Critical Approaches to the Novel* [1967]) shows how much it is defined by her style, as plain and devoid of ornament as her dress. In this
whole chapter there are not a dozen similes or metaphors, none of them
in Dorothea's speech or thought. The only ones in Ladislaw's are his
brief outburst: 'It is as fatal as murder or any other horror that divides
people; ... it is more intolerable — to have our life maimed by petty
accidents.' All the other images occur in the author's commentary:
' "You acted as I should have expected you to act," said Dorothea, her
face brightening and her head becoming a little more erect on its beautiful stem." ' Or 'the flood of her young passion bearing down all ob-
structions.' Two of them describe Will: with hat and gloves in hand he
'might have done for the portrait of a Royalist,' and he started up 'as if
some torture-screw were upon him.' The relative calm of the lovers'
dialogue contrasts with the wild storm outside, which expresses their

turbulent emotion. This is one of the most ancient romantic devices. Fires flashed in the heavens when Dido and Aeneas found themselves together in the cave; Scott, Dickens, the Brontës, Thackeray, Meredith, Hardy, and many later novelists have used it, usually for melodramatic effect. It is handled with restraint in *Middlemarch*. Dorothea darted from the window when the vivid flash of lightning came, and Will, following, seized her hand with a spasmodic movement, 'and so they stood, with their hands clasped, like two children looking out at the storm.' At the very end, after Will has declared that his poverty would keep him from offering himself to any woman 'even if she had no luxuries to renounce,' Dorothea says: 'I don't mind about poverty − I hate my wealth,' adding 'in a sobbing childlike way,' 'We could live quite well on my own fortune − it is too much − seven hundred a-year − I want so little − no new clothes − and I will learn what everything costs' (83:594). At the very climax of emotion the irony that George Eliot has focused throughout on Dorothea's immaturity is not allowed to lapse.

Henry James was one of the first critics to feel that Ladislaw was lacking in masculinity. 'If Dorothea had married any one after her misadventure with Casaubon,' he wrote, 'she would have married a hussar!'

He is, we may say, the one figure which a masculine intellect of the power as George Eliot's would not have conceived with the same complacency; he is, in short, roughly speaking, a woman's man ...

We are doubtless less content with Ladislaw, on account of the noble, almost sculptural, relief of the neighboring figure of Lydgate, the real hero of the story.[11]

The glamour of the 'noble, almost sculptural' figure of the 'real hero' was felt by others besides James, whose homo-erotic attraction to vigorous young men Leon Edel has documented. Even before the final books of *Middlemarch* were published many readers speculated hopefully that Dorothea and Lydgate might marry as a compensation for their earlier matrimonial trials. The *Saturday Review* exclaimed: 'poor Lydgate − ten times the better man − suffers not only in happiness, but in his noblest ambitions, and sinks to the lower level of a good practice and a good income because he marries and is faithful to the vain selfish creature whom Ladislaw merely flirts with.'[12] This opinion misrepresents Ladislaw's relations with Rosamond and assigns her more than her share of blame for Lydgate's failure. From his first appearance in the story George Eliot has indicated the major weakness in Lydgate's character: he could recognize the pink stage of typhoid fever, but was blind to his own susceptibility to blue eyes. Even the melodramatic episode with Madame Laure had not taught him much. Edith Simcox perceived that he

is one of those men whose lives are cut in two, whose intellectual interests have no direct connection with their material selves, and who only discover the impossibility of living according to habit or tradition when brought by accident or their own heedlessness face to face with difficulties that require thought as well as resolution. There was not room in the life he contemplated for a soul much larger than Rosamond's, and it may be doubted whether the Rosamond he wished for would not, by a merely passive influence, have been as obstructive to his wide speculations ... On the other hand, if the scientific ardour had been more absorbing, he might have gone on his own way, crushing all poor Rosamond's little schemes of opposition, and then she would have been the victim instead of the oppressor, but his character would have been as far from ideal excellence as before.[13]

Despite his weakness Lydgate is more appealing than Ladislaw – as Samson tamed by Delilah is more appealing than Joseph resisting Potiphar's wife. But there is no blurring the tragic fact that Lydgate's failure came from his own slackening resolution. His idea of a wife's function was little better than Casaubon's: 'to cast a charm over vacant hours' (5:32). Even James' 'nobly strenuous' Dorothea might have found marriage with Lydgate disastrous. His massive frame and large white hands are in marked contrast with Ladislaw's slim figure and long thin fingers, inherited from aristocratic Polish ancestors. In spite of his girlish complexion there is nothing effeminate in Will's fiery response to Raffles, as he turns 'like a tiger-cat ready to spring on him,' making that overbearing bully draw back (60:446). The notion that masculinity is proportional to bodily weight is a common but questionable male dogma.

W.J. Harvey thought that George Eliot failed with the Dorothea-Will relationship because she was 'unwilling or unable to treat fully and properly ... romantic or passionate love between two adults.'[14] If there were such a failure, I believe it must be judged in the context of its time. Not lack of willingness or ability, but the circulating library, the shilling magazine, and the general custom of family reading imposed this reticence on all the Victorian novelists. 'The death-bed might be public, but not the marriage bed,' wrote Kathleen Tillotson in her *Novels of the Eighteen-Forties* (1954, p 54), the best account I know of that aspect of the nineteenth-century novel. Its problem was to convey the idea of passion to adult readers in terms that would not 'bring a blush into the cheek of the young person.' Neither magazine nor circulating library would countenance candid treatment of sexual relations. To compare George Eliot with Flaubert or Tolstoy, to say that one cannot imagine her 'encompassing ... the complex intensities of Anna Karenina's passion' is hardly fair. Tolstoy read all George Eliot's novels, most of them in the year they were published. There were five editions of *Middlemarch* in Russian before 1875, when *Anna Karenina* appeared, and its influence on Tolstoy has never been adequately studied. Had George Eliot been writing in France or Russia her account of the Casaubon honeymoon would have been more explicit, and Ladislaw's thought of Dorothea might not have been screened behind tall lilies. But in England the 'troughs of Zolaism' and the conviction of Vizetelly for publishing *La Terre* were still eighteen years in the future. We ought rather to compare Dorothea and Ladislaw with Bella Wilfer and John Harmon in *Our Mutual Friend* (1864-5) or Zoë and Lord Uxmoor in Reade's *A Woman Hater* (1874) — a needless task — or any of Trollope's young lovers, or those in Hardy's early novels.

Pace Henry James, the true hero of *Middlemarch* is Will Ladislaw. A serious obstacle to Lydgate's candidacy which rarely occurs to modern readers is the wide difference in rank between a lady in county society and a surgeon. Today, when medical men enjoy perhaps a higher respect than clergymen, we can hardly conceive what a lowly position they held in 1830. In the houses of great people, then, 'if it was necessary to offer [them] a meal, [they were] entertained in the steward's or housekeeper's room.'[15] In choosing his profession Lydgate had stepped below his rank, flouting the traditions of his family, and he descended even further in marrying the granddaughter of an innkeeper. The Lydgates of Quallingham would probably have agreed with Mrs Cadwallader's generalization that 'the people in manufacturing towns are always disreputable.' As the orphan son of a penniless military man, the younger brother of a baronet in the north, Lydgate's pretensions to rank were not imposing. We are liable to view them through Rosamond's dazzled eyes. We also tend to underestimate Ladislaw's position as a gentleman. His grandfather, bearing the name of the greatest Polish king, was a patriot who fled to the West after the first partition of Poland in 1772. Though George Eliot does not give him a title, he was obviously cultivated, 'a bright fellow — could speak many languages — musical — got his bread by teaching all sorts of things.' From him Will's father inherited the musical talent and the aristocratic hands; from his mother came the grey eyes and the 'delicate irregular nose with the little ripple in it,' which he passed on to his son. Will's mother, Sarah Dunkirk, a pretty, proud-spirited lass, well educated in a fine boarding school, was, according to Raffles, 'fit for a lord's wife.' On learning the criminal character of her father's business, Sarah had run away from home and gone on the stage. Of course these low connections constitute a blemish on Will's pedigree. Yet a woman always takes her husband's rank; the peerage is studded with noblemen whose mothers had dubious origin and made their debuts in the theatre. [16]

In the English novel, where the law of primogeniture is not often set aside, the inheritance of property plays an important part in the plot. Tom Jones, illegitimate but older than Blifil, inherits Allworthy's estate and, by the hand of Sophia, Squire Western's too. In Gothic novels the hero invariably proves to be the heir to the castle. Mr Knightley in winning Emma Woodhouse for his wife returns Hartfield to the Donwell Abbey estate, of which it was originally a part. In Scott's novels a regular feature is the ultimate junction of hero with real estate, which he secures, not by killing his enemy in a duel, but through his legal right of inheritance. Alexander Welsh demonstrates in *The Hero of the Waverley Novels* (1963) how the so-called passive heroes — unlike the Fergus MacIvors, Rob Roys, and Redgauntlets — abstain from violence because as English gentlemen they rely on the law, which always vindicates them. We can trace something of this pattern in George Eliot, who from childhood was nourished on Scott's novels. Many of his heroes are mild, dreamy youths, thrown by chance into adventures in which they play largely passive roles. For example, Frank Osbaldistone, the only son of an elder son, is a rebellious dilettante, interested chiefly in poetry, a drop-out from a business career with his father, who in his own youth had abandoned his rank by going into trade in London, yielding the title and the family estates in the North to his younger brother. At the end of the tale, more through the initiative of Rob Roy and Di Vernon than by his own efforts, Frank is restored to his proper place as head of the family and lord of Osbaldistone Hall.

We see a certain parallel in the case of Will Ladislaw. His grandmother, Casaubon's Aunt Julia, was the elder and prettier of the two ladies of Lowick Manor. When she was disinherited for her mésalliance, the estate passed to her younger sister, who married a Mr Casaubon and had two sons. The elder inherited the estate; the younger, Edward, became a clergyman and lived at Lowick parsonage until, on the death of his brother about 1819, he took possession of the manor. The history of Casaubon's family is very shadowy. He told Dorothea that he had 'none but comparatively distant connections' (37:274); we hear from Cadwallader that he 'is very good to his poor relations: pensions several of the women' (8:51); but we never see any of them – in curious contrast with the presumptive heirs of Peter Featherstone. Will Ladislaw's father was one of these poor relations towards whom Mr Casaubon recognized a duty and, having learned of his desperate plight, ill and starving at Boulogne, sent him money, and after his death continued the allowance to his widow and son Will, whose education he paid for.

Dorothea, with whom generous feelings often took precedence of practical realities, regarded the disinheriting of Aunt Julia as a cruel injustice, and thought that Will – the sole descendant of the elder branch of the family – had an equal claim to the estate. With the ardour that often supplanted her tact she broached the matter at night during one of Mr Casaubon's sleepless intervals, urging Will's claim to half the property settled on her before her marriage, with an immediate provision for him on that understanding. As George Eliot points out, Dorothea 'was blind to many things obvious to others – likely to tread in the wrong places' (37:273), of which this was certainly one. Ironically, her well-meant effort for Ladislaw, who would never himself have dreamed of such a claim, precipitated Casaubon's codicil depriving them both of the estate.[17]

In the elaborate plot of *Middlemarch*, which the Victorians so much enjoyed, Ladislaw with his relation to Casaubon and to Bulstrode, his employment by Mr Brooke, and his involvement with the Lydgates provides the only coherent focus. Through his mother Will has a similar moral claim on the Dunkirk fortune. After the death of her only son and her husband, Mrs Dunkirk, who never knew the precise nature of the pawnbroker's business, tried earnestly to find Sarah. Only after all efforts had failed did she consent to marry the confidential accountant, young Brother Bulstrode, whose piety in prayer meetings had made her trust him. But she was deceived. The daughter had been found by Raffles, whom Bulstrode bribed to silence and shipped off to New York. Except for this concealment the Dunkirk money would have been Sarah's, and Will Ladislaw might never have come to Lowick. 'But the train of causes in which [Bulstrode] had locked himself went on." During nearly thirty years of philanthropy at Middlemarch he had striven vainly to convince himself that his good works justified the fraud by which he had got the Ladislaws' money. Then, when Raffles threatens exposure, Bulstrode asked Will to call on him and told him of the marriage to Mrs Dunkirk, which had enriched him. 'So far as human laws go, you have no claim on me whatever,' he said; yet there was a claim his conscience recognized. Accordingly he offered Will an income of £500 a year and support for any laudable plan he might have in prospect. Will's rejection of the offer is merciless:

'My unblemished honour is important to me. It is important to me to have no stain on my birth and connections. And now I find there is a stain which I can't help. My mother felt it, and tried to keep as clear of it as she could, and so will I. You shall keep your ill-gotten money. If I had any fortune of my own, I would willingly pay it to any one who could disprove what you have told me. What I have to thank you for is that you kept the money till now, when I can refuse it. It ought to lie with a man's self that he is a gentleman. Good-night, sir.'

It is an impressive scene, quietly handled, with none of the florid rhetoric in which Dickens would have decked it. George Eliot examines the tangled feelings underlying Will's bitter words. In the rush of his impulses 'there was mingled the sense that it would have been impossible for him ever to tell Dorothea that he had accepted it.'

Bulstrode's emotions are also analyzed with the same sympathetic understanding that his creator extends to good and bad alike.[18]

Perhaps it is only heroes of romance who spurn offers of £500 a year so scornfully. The typical villain, like Monks in *Oliver Twist*, is usually forced in a melodramatic exposure to disgorge the hero's property and betake himself to prison or the Antipodes. But *Middlemarch* is no romance. Bulstrode is allowed to keep the money which would have made Will independent. To marry him Dorothea gives up the Casaubon estate — possibly to those shadowy pensioners; we can never know. Middlemarch tradition declared that she gave it up to marry a man 'with no property and not well-born,' and it was usually said that she could not have been 'a nice woman.' Though Mr Brooke corresponded with them, for a long time he did not invite the Ladislaws to the Grange. He talked a good deal about cutting off the entail so that his estate, which was worth £3,000 a year, could go to Celia's son and join Tipton with the well-kept farms of Freshitt. But after Dorothea's son was born, Sir James advised Mr Brooke to let the entail alone. And so the young Ladislaw will grow up to inherit the Tipton estate and fulfil the role of fictional hero, which in a romance would have been his father's.

Will became an ardent public man, working well in those times when reforms were begun with a young hopefulness of immediate good which has been much checked in our days and getting at last returned to Parliament by a constituency who paid his expenses. (Finale:610-11).

Cynics are sometimes sceptical of this career. Leslie Stephen (possibly glancing at G.H. Lewes) thought it would be easy to suggest a living original for some of Will's peculiarities, but could not believe that he ever got into parliament.

Ladislaw, I am convinced, became a brilliant journalist who could write smartly about everything, but who had not the moral force to be a leader in thought or action. I should be the last person to deny that a journalist may lead an honourable and useful life, but I cannot think the profession congenial to a lofty devotion to ideals. Dorothea was content with giving him 'wifely help'; asking his friends to dinner, one supposes, and copying his ill-written manuscripts.[19]

Stephen's sarcasm was hardly called for. Dorothea never repented that
she had married Ladislaw. 'They were bound to each other by a love
stronger than any impulses which could have marred it' (Finale:610).
Joan Bennett sums the matter up wisely and with moderation:

Marriage with Ladislaw is not meant to be the fulfilment of Dorothea's
youthful dreams ... [It] is an improvement on the first because its basis
is an appreciation of the man as he is; their love for each other com-
prises mutual sympathy, understanding and respect ... Dorothea invents
no fiction about Ladislaw nor he about her ... The reader discerns faults,
weaknesses or irritating tricks in Ladislaw which, he supposes, would
alienate her.

But, Mrs Bennett continues tolerantly, this was not the opinion of perceptive people like Lydgate and the Farebrothers, who like him very
much. And he

has certain qualities which were particularly likely to attract Dorothea
after her experience with Casaubon. He is spontaneous and unselfcon-
scious; he responds to beauty in art or nature and to nobility in human
character with romantic ardour. His intelligence is quick and gay — a
happy contrast to Casaubon's ponderous learning. His nature is in many
ways complementary to her own. Certainly George Eliot did not intend
us to share Sir James Chettam's view that their marriage was a disaster.[20]

So let us end with Dorothea's warm words: 'I will not hear any evil
spoken of Mr Ladislaw; he has already suffered too much injustice'
(62:460).

NOTES

1 Arthur Ponsonby *Henry Ponsonby* (1942) 259, and Algernon West
   Recollections (1900) 281
2 'George Eliot's *Middlemarch*,' in *Galaxy* 15 (March 1873) 426
3 *The Great Tradition: George Eliot, Henry James, Joseph Conrad* (1948) 75
4 *Middlemarch* xii-xiii.
5 References in this paragraph are as follows: 34:231; 84:599; 9:58; 9:59;
   21:152; 60:466; 19:140.

6 *The George Eliot Letters* G.S. Haight ed (New Haven 1954-5) III 274
7 References in this paragraph are as follows: 21:153; 21:154; 46:377; 37:269; 39:286.
8 *Saturday Review* (7 December 1872) 734
9 *The Great Tradition* 76
10 George Eliot wrote (82:589) 'had been in a world apart.' By omitting 'as' in quoting the passage Dr Leavis blurs the metaphorical nature of Ladislaw's thoughts.
11 *'Daniel Deronda*: A Conversation,' in *Atlantic Monthly* 38 (December 1876) 690, and 'George Eliot's *Middlemarch*,' in *Galaxy* 15 (March 1873) 426
12 *Saturday Review* 734
13 *Academy* 4 (1 January 1873) 3
14 *The Art of George Eliot* (1961) 197
15 G.M. Young, ed, *Early Victorian England* (1934) I 96
16 References in this paragraph are as follows: 62:460; 37:268; 9:58; 60:447.
17 Though George Eliot was always obsessively anxious about the legal details in her novels, there is nothing in her papers or notebooks concerning this codicil. Had Dorothea deigned to contest it, would the court have set it aside, particularly since Will Ladislaw was Casaubon's nearest blood relation? In *The George Eliot Letters* (II 319-20) I noted the parallel between Casaubon's will and that in the case of Branwell Brontë, who, according to Mrs Gaskell, was dismissed as tutor in the family of the Reverend Edmund Robinson because of the 'criminal advances' made to him by Mrs Robinson. In the *Life of Charlotte Brontë* (1st ed 1857, I 226) Mrs Gaskell declared that the Reverend Mr Robinson altered his will to bequeath his property to his wife 'solely on the condition that she should never see Branwell Brontë again.' Threatened with a libel suit, Mrs Gaskell made a public apology in a letter to *The Times* (30 May 1857, 5b), retracted every statement imputing any breach of conjugal duties or 'guilty intercourse with the late Branwell Brontë,' and removed the offensive passages from the revised edition. Mr Robinson's will contains no reference to Branwell, who was probably dismissed for some indiscretion with his pupil, thirteen-year-old Edmund Robinson, Jr. George Eliot read Mrs Gaskell's book as soon as it appeared and was deeply moved by it but regretted her setting down Branwell's alcoholism and addiction to opium as due entirely to his remorse over the alleged affair with Mrs Robinson, which 'would not make such a life as Branwell's was in the last three or four years unless the germs of vice had sprouted and shot up long before.'
18 References in this paragraph are to chapter 61:451, 455, 457.
19 *George Eliot* (1906) 179-80
20 *George Eliot: Her Mind and Her Art* (1948) 176-7

U. C. KNOEPFLMACHER

Fusing fact and myth:
the new reality of *Middlemarch*

In chapter 27 of *Middlemarch*, Tertius Lydgate and Rosamond Vincy
thumb through the pages of the last issue of ' "Keepsake," the gor-
geous water-silk publication which marked modern progress at that
time.' The journal has been given to Rosamond by her admirer Ned
Plymdale, 'one of the good matches in Middlemarch, though not one
of its leading minds.' Eager to show his mental superiority to poor
Ned, Lydgate draws the magazine towards him and gives a 'short scorn-
ful laugh,' while tossing up 'his chin, as in wonderment at human folly.'
He finds the writing as trite as the engravings; mockingly, he says to
Rosamond: 'Do look at this bridegroom coming out of a church: did
you ever see such a "sugared invention" – as the Elizabethans used to
say?'

   There is an obvious cluster of ironies in this passage, for Lydgate is,
of course, in the very process of yielding to the bourgeois adornments
he so scornfully derides. Although he may hold himself superior in education and in refinement to Ned Plymdale, he is about to replace the
donor of *Keepsake* as Rosamond's most unthinking worshiper. The
journal's reproduction of contemporary caprice may strike Lydgate as
an example of 'human folly,' but the narrator has already told us in
this very same chapter that the doctor has found in neither 'folly' nor
his 'science' an antidote against the surface charms which Ned, too,
finds so irresistible. Lydgate thus is about to adopt the very mindless-
ness he indicts. As a bridegroom soon to emerge from church with

Rosamond at his hand, he gives a new twist to the text in the magazine; the picture and story he mocks — of a 'smirking' groom who thinks himself 'one of the first gentlemen in the land' — will become a kind of *memento mori* for his own aspirations, his desire 'to do good small work for Middlemarch, and great work for the world' (15:110).

Unlike Dorothea Brooke, who, 'by the side of provincial fashion' retains the distinction of 'a fine quotation from the Bible, — or from one of our elder poets, — in a paragraph of to-day's newspaper' (1:5), Lydgate succumbs to the petty particulars of provincial life. The would-be discoverer hoped to bring a new 'light' to the still 'dark territories of Pathology,' sure that his discovery of 'new connections and hitherto hidden facts of structure' would help him enlarge the 'scientific, rational basis of his profession.' Instead, however, he finds himself yielding to the ephemeral notion of 'progress' epitomized by *Keepsake* magazine. Once eager to soar with no middle flight above the mundane and the everyday, Lydgate becomes grounded by Middlemarch. Like Ned Plymdale — or like the object-less Mr Brooke — he becomes a 'middle marcher,' a creature who lives for the present only because he is incapable of channeling the energy that would convert that present into a conduit between past and future.

So much for the obvious ironies involved in the scene in chapter 27. But what about Lydgate's curious use of an Elizabethan phrase, 'sugared invention,' within the confines of the Vincys' drawing room? Does the phrase carry some meaning that he does not quite fathom, and, if so, what are the 'new connections and hitherto hidden facts of structure' that George Eliot wants us to see? To understand the import of the allusion, we will have to indulge in a little literary detective-work.

In 1868, after the publication of her long epic poem *The Spanish Gypsy*, George Eliot began to consider new themes for shorter poems, as well as for longer works, either of poetry or of prose. In the fall of 1868 she embarked on a rereading of English poetry from its beginnings, using both Thomas Warton's *The History of English Poetry* and Edwin Guest's *History of English Rhythms* as guides. Almost at the same time, she began to read George Grote's eight-volume *History of Greece*. Although by 1 January of 1869 she already lists the 'novel called Middlemarch' among her projects for that year, she seems to have been diverted by her desire to work on 'a long poem on Timoleon, and several minor poems.'[1] Consequently, her extensive reading in medical subjects, in works such as Renouard's *History of Medicine from its Origins to the Nineteenth Century* and J.R. Russell's *The History and Heroes of the Art of Medicine*, does not seem to have begun until the middle of 1869, around the time that she began in earnest the story of the Vincys, Featherstone, and the young doctor called Lydgate.

In the fall of 1868, however, the Lydgate who interested George Eliot was still a poet — John Lydgate, Chaucer's successor. She recorded several extracts from *The Fall of Princes* in the 1868-71 Notebook now at the Folger Library and seems to have been drawn to the particulars of his life. Her interest was apparently stimulated by Warton's high praise for Lydgate's contributions to the 'amplification of our language' and by the poet's encyclopaedic knowledge; moreover, as Colonel John Pratt, the editor of the Folger Notebook, persuasively demonstrates, she was apparently struck by the oblivion into which Lydgate — whose very name may have been unknown to her up to this point — had fallen: whereas Warton in the eighteenth century accorded the poet a pre-eminent place, Guest in the nineteenth century all but dismisses his work.[2]

George Eliot's readings in Grote's *History of Greece* illustrate a parallel interest. Fascinated by the story of Timoleon, she started 'meditating' it as a 'subject' as early as 22 November 1868.[3] The Corinthian leader who had freed the Syracusans from the oppression of Carthage was another advanced figure forgotten by history and resting in an unvisited tomb. His failure to raise even 'one memorial hope' during the era of the French Revolution had already been deplored by Wordsworth in book X of *The Prelude*.[4] Warton and Grote thus simultaneously stimulated George Eliot's concern with figures thwarted by the passage of time: Lydgate the neglected poet and Timoleon the neglected political reformer.

What is more, Warton and Grote also sharpened another interest that soon was to become a fuller preoccupation: both writers, in tracing sources, suggested that an intimate correlation between historical fact and mythical fable existed in early periods of poetry. Thus, Warton admits that it is impossible to distinguish between historical truth and fiction in the *Gesta Romanorum* because in an age of 'vision' in which every work 'was believed to contain a double or secondary meaning'

no such distinctions had been made; similarly, Grote credits Theagenes
of Rhegium for starting 'the idea of a double meaning in the Homeric
and Hesiodic narratives' and refers his readers to Milton's own blurring
of fable and history in *Paradise Lost,* a work which George Eliot duti-
fully reread around this time.[5]

Her simultaneous readings in Greek subjects and in the literatures of
the Middle Ages and the Renaissance also seems to have sharpened
George Eliot's ever-ready eye for comparisons and analogies. For example, under the heading of 'Kinship of the Medieval and Classic,' she
juxtaposes in her Notebook events taken from the myth of Theseus
and their counterparts in Spanish chivalric romances.[6] It is this same
interest in comparisons and cross-references which therefore may have
originally stimulated the entry recorded on page 14 of her Notebook:
' "Sugared invention" (Frances Meres of Theagines + Chariclea).' She
follows this citation with another: 'As Italy had Dante +c ... So England
had Matthew Royden +c ...'[7] and then gives the title of the work from
which both of these citations are taken: 'A Comparative Discourse of
our English Poets with the Greek, Latin & Italian Poets,' by Frances
Meres, MA, 1598. She had obviously come across the work better
known as *Palladis Tamia*, either in Grote or, more likely, in Warton.
Clearly she wanted to remember the name of the man who had thought
of exalting one Matthew Royden as England's Dante. But Meres himself
must have been of considerably less interest to her than the context of
the phrase, 'sugared invention.' In drawing up his analogies between
English poets and their Greek, Latin, and Italian counterparts Meres
was actually touching upon a subject of deep concern to George Eliot
in 1868 – namely, the relation between poetry and prose.

In the pertinent passage in *Palladis Tamia* in which the phrase
'sugared invention' occurs, Francis Meres slavishly copies the ideas expressed in a far more important Elizabethan critical manifesto, Sir Philip
Sidney's 'Defence of Poesy' and renders these ideas in Sidney's exact
wording. It was Sidney who had first asserted that verse was 'but an
ornament and no cause to poetry, sith there have been many most excellent poets that never versified ... For Xenophon, who did imitate so
excellently as to give us *effigiem justi imperii* – the portraiture of a just
empire, under the name of Cyrus (as Cicero saith of him) made therein
an absolute heroical poem; so did Heliodorus in his sugared invention of

that picture of love in Theagenes and Chariclea; and yet both of these writ in prose.'[8] Meres repeats Sidney's argument and phrasing. He, too, asserts that Xenophon and Heliodorus, both 'excellent admired poets,' in the *Cyropaedia* and in *Theagenes and Chariclea*, respectively, achieved in prose what others achieved in poetry; Meres' only departure from the original comparison consists of his adding one native English writer to the list —none other than his source, Sir Philip Sidney himself, who, Meres enthusiastically avows, 'writ his immortal poem, the Countess of Pembroke's Arcadia in prose; and yet our rarest poet.'[9]

The phrase that Lydgate so casually tosses out in chapter 27 in *Middlemarch* thus turns out to have a rather venerable ancestry. Moreover, its use in George Eliot's novel is, I think, rather significant. Its significance does not just lie in the fact that in *Middlemarch* George Eliot should allude both to Xenophon's *Cyropaedia* and to Sidney's *Arcadia*,[10] or that her Notebook should contain a further reference to 'The Defence of Poesy,'[11] and also call attention to Theagenes of Rhegium, who believed that mythological narratives ought to convey 'an interior sense, different from that which the words on their obvious meaning bore, yet to a certain extent analogous, and discoverable by sagacious divination.'[12] Instead, the fullest significance of the phrase lies in its relation to George Eliot's emerging views about the nature of poetic form and to her dissatisfaction with the imitative realism she had practiced in her earlier fiction. Let me explain.

The George Eliot who, in 1868, envisioned *Timoleon* as a long companion piece to *The Spanish Gypsy*, and who, in 1869 and 1870, worked on the shorter poems, 'Agatha,' 'Lisa,' 'Jubal,' 'Armgart,' as well as the 'Brother and Sister' sonnets, had turned to poetry because she regarded it as a form less restricted to a faithful reproduction of the outlines of the external world. Her readings in Warton and Grote and in Max Müller the linguist gradually allowed her to see that she could do in a work of prose fiction what in her 'Notes on Form in Art' she suggested that poetry alone could do: transcend the limitations imposed on the natural historian. In that extraordinary essay (written in 1868 but first printed by Thomas Pinney in 1963), George Eliot argues that poetry can convey truths higher than those attained by Harvey and Bichat (Lydgate, it ought to be remembered, is first stimulated by Harvey and then tries to model his career after the precedent of Bichat).

Form, George Eliot asserts, must first depend on discriminations, on the recognition of unlikeness and difference. Only after smaller and smaller unlikenesses have been recognized, can a conception of wholes be gained — 'wholes composed of parts more and more multiplied and highly differenced, yet more and more absolutely bound together by various conditions of common likeness or mutual dependence.'[13]

In *Middlemarch* — a novel which originated in a fusion of unlike parts — George Eliot puts on trial Lydgate's empiricist view of reality. To the physician, words are vague, less trustworthy than the microscope. In a conversation with Bulstrode, Lydgate seizes on the banker's use of the phrase 'spiritual interests' by saying, 'those words are apt to cover different meanings to different minds.' Lydgate prefers to reduce reality to its smallest and — as he thinks — precisest, components by 'diligent application, not only of the scalpel, but of the microscope.'[14] A votary of 'scientific culture' who adheres to 'the philosophy of medical evidence,' he is particularly distrustful of the vagueness of that 'sugared invention' which feigns or distorts. And yet, ironically enough, Lydgate has in the past already once been fooled by a fiction. The melodrama staged by the Provençale actress Laure appealed to his fancy. Relying on that fancy (rather than imagination), Lydgate was led to sentimentalize reality: 'all science had come to a stand-still while he imagined the unhappy Laure, stricken by ever-wandering sorrow, herself wandering, and finding no comforter.' His sentimentalization, the fiction he has concocted, comes to an abrupt halt when he discovers the truth; chastened, he returns to his laboratory, believing that 'illusions were at an end for him.' He is determined henceforth to take a 'strictly scientific view of woman.'[15]

By putting Sidney's phrase into the mouth of Lydgate, of all characters, George Eliot wants us to recognize the limitations of the man with a forgotten poet's name. Unlike the Ladislaw who defends language as a 'finer medium' for its ability to capture those essences or forms that a painting or sculpture can only represent through an external copy, Lydgate never learns to see beneath 'mere coloured superficies.' He mistakes copies for truth and confuses ornament for essence. On first listening to Dorothea speak, Lydgate dismisses her because he finds fault with her unclever words: 'It is troublesome to talk to such women.' By way of contrast, Ladislaw, who has met Dorothea in the previous chapter, is quick to separate her 'words' (which he finds *too* clever) from her musical voice.: 'But what a voice! It was like the voice of a soul that had once lived in an Æolian harp.' A similar separation is made by Caleb Garth much later. Reporting on his conversation with Dorothea to his wife, he says: 'You would like to hear her speak, Susan. She speaks in such plain words, and a voice like music.' Ladislaw and Caleb Garth recognize what Lydgate fails to see. Although the one is the cosmopolitan grandson of a man who could speak 'many languages — musical' and the other an ineloquent carpenter, both men revere music. Both identify Dorothea with the 'structure of tones' which George Eliot regards as the highest form of art and which in her 'Notes on Form' she equates with the highest modes of poetry. Lydgate, however, lacks the ear to distinguish between the music of the senses and the music of the soul. His own 'sugared invention' leads him to falsify Rosamond into a water-nixie whose melodious sea-breezes will, he hopes, only strengthen his work at the microscope.[16]

It is fitting that this scoffer at the imprecision of words should later be punished by Rosamond's willful silence. Although his private canary bird warbles back at him, there is neither soul nor understanding in her song. If Lydgate becomes the victim of his own, inferior 'sugared invention,' George Eliot, however, opposes her own powers of invention to his. Through the Elizabethan phrase she puts into his mouth, she creates what Sidney calls a 'speaking picture,' a 'figuring forth' of reality, that allows us to divine meanings which Lydgate the diagnostician cannot fathom. 'How often,' says Sidney in his 'Defence,' 'think you, do the physicians lie, when they aver things good for sickness ... Now for the poet, he nothing affirmeth, and therefore he never lieth.'[17] Years ago, in *Religious Humanism and the Victorian Novel*, I cited this passage to show how the views of reality figured forth by Lydgate and Ladislaw, physician and poet, are contrasted in *Middlemarch*. And indeed, George Eliot seems to approve of Ladislaw's contention that language alone can render a fuller image, 'which is all the better for being vague.' Ladislaw's view that the 'true seeing is within' (19:142), is in direct variance with Lydgate's too rigid perception of truth.

But my present object is not to contrast the imaginations of Lydgate and Ladislaw, but rather to look at some of the characteristics of the imagination that shaped *Middlemarch*. I have started out with Lydgate because he not only is the foil of Dorothea and Ladislaw, but is also very much the foil of George Eliot herself. And Lydgate is George Eliot's foil, because — like all those other characters in the novel who try to impose their mental structures on reality — he is engaged in the same quest as the novelist. Lydgate wants to demonstrate the 'more intimate relations of living structure, and help to define men's thought more accurately after the true order' (15:110). George Eliot's aims in this work are identical: she wants to demonstrate more intimate relations within the reality she creates and so help define her readers' thoughts more accurately after a truer order — an order which partakes both of fact and of myth.

What I am saying, then, is this: in *Middlemarch* the artist is a participant in the very same process of ordering that her characters are engaged in. Yet whereas the structures erected by a Lydgate, a Casaubon, a Dorothea, or a Bulstrode prove to be too fixed, it is the richly allusive medium of language which the novelist employs that allows her to discover a more complex and multiform order of meaning. What George Eliot has to say about 'poetry' in her 'Notes on Form in Art' thus very definitely applies to the mode she came to develop in *Middlemarch*: 'poetry, from being the fullest expression of the human soul, is starved into an ingenious pattern-work, in which tricks with vocables take the place of living words fed with the blood of relevant meaning, and [are] made musical by the continual intercommunication of sensibility and thought.'[18] By fusing history and fiction, the prosaic and the poetic, the factual and the mythological, George Eliot blurs through the superiority of her own 'sugared invention' the fixities which her main characters adopt. Words, vocables, 'the old phrases,' asserts George Eliot toward the end of her essay, should not have to 'give way to scientific explanation.' Instead, they can carry meanings that defy empirical classification — whether that classification be Casaubon's pigeon-holing of myths he has emptied of their affective content or Lydgate's false separation of matter and essence.

Middlemarch did replace the long poem on Timoleon that George Eliot had projected. Yet it was in *Middlemarch* that George Eliot put into practice the ideas about poetic form she had developed. The fusion of two 'parts' totally 'differenced' — a novella about a latter-day Puritan's aspirations and a study of a thwarted physician's life in the provinces — led her to the recognition that she could integrate smaller and smaller parts, all carefully differentiated, by creating new 'conditions of common likeness or mutual dependence.' These conditions of likeness were no longer confined exclusively to the strict mimetic rules the novelist had previously observed. In *Middlemarch* George Eliot still employs the precise spatial and temporal frames so characteristic of her earlier work; yet she also depends on connotations such as one finds in poetry. Hilda M. Hulme has recently shown[19] how the novel's imagery creates metaphoric associations that are far more complicated than those found in any of George Eliot's previous fictions. The novel's dense network of allusion acts as an equally important associational device. As we shall see, Lydgate's faulty application of an old Elizabethan phrase is but one of many elaborate ironies created through allusions that, at first, seem cryptic or arbitrary, but which, on closer inspection, reveal that they have been most carefully woven into the 'ingenious pattern-work' called *Middlemarch.*

II

Chapter 1 of the novel first introduces us to the character of the Reverend Edward Casaubon. Yet we meet Casaubon by hearsay only. The narrator tells us that Dorothea feels 'some venerating expectation' about the gentleman about to dine at the Grange and then proceeds to render an intentionally vague picture of the expected visitor by forcing us to see him through the limited eyes of the county. With an ambivalence calculated to raise our own expectations, the narrator soon drops the subject altogether and turns to Dorothea's search for 'the keys, the keys' to the cabinet into which she had locked her mother's jewels. Rather unhelpfully, the narrator says about Mr Casaubon: 'His very name carried an impressiveness hardly to be measured without a precise chronology of scholarship.'

In his excellent essay on 'Casaubon and Lydgate,' the late W.J. Harvey noted the parallelism between the intellectual aspirations of Casaubon and Lydgate and correctly pointed out that both men are the vehicles of George Eliot's profound suspicion 'of anything in the nature of *a* key to the meaning of life.'[20] Lydgate's desire to trace all life to a single cellular archetype and Casaubon's search for a single fountainhead for all mythologies are products of a similar conception of reality. Professor Harvey demonstrated this in his careful reconstruction of the extensive research into comparative mythology and biology that George Eliot undertook before she drew Casaubon and Lydgate. Fearful, however, that his research might ultimately have been 'extrinsic' to the dramatic effects of the novel itself, Professor Harvey apologized for dealing with material that 'may seem irrelevant' to the novel's readers. His fear was unnecessary. Had he lived long enough to study the Folger Notebook edited by Colonel Pratt, he would, I am convinced, have felt less apologetic for the kind of documentation he provided in his essay as well as in the footnotes to his edition of the novel.

As John Pratt demonstrates again and again, George Eliot did not at all forgo material such as that which she unearthed in his investigation of Casaubon's intellectual *milieu*. Quite to the contrary, her tendency was to appropriate this material and make it a part of her fable. When the narrator invites us to measure the impressiveness of Casaubon's name by relying on a 'precise chronology of scholarship,' he is, among other things, preparing us for Mr Casaubon's own inability to move beyond the eighteenth-century scholarship of men like Jacob Bryant, the mythographer who tried to 'divest Tradition of Fable, and to restore Truth to its Original Purity.'[21]

From Knight's *Cyclopaedia*, a work on which she relied for many biographical facts in the composition of *Middlemarch*, George Eliot apparently discovered that Bryant suffered from a 'complaint in the eyes' and that he died in consequence of a freakish accident which resulted in a 'hurt which he received in the leg by a chair slipping from under him while taking down a book from an upper shelf.'[22] Such details are appropriated in *Middlemarch* and assimilated into the novel's metaphorical ironies: Casaubon's complaint that he has been using up his 'eyesight' leads the myopic Dorothea to desire that she may become a 'lamp-holder' for the man she identifies with the blind Milton, yet whose 'small taper' is soon seen in all its insignificance at the residence called Lowick; similarly, in chapter 29, Casaubon's weak legs — repeatedly deplored by Sir James — and his even weaker heart — soon diagnosed by Lydgate as suffering from a fatty 'degeneration' — cause him to stumble on the library-steps on which he is perched to pick up a book: only Dorothea's quick intervention and *her* tender heart

prevent the bookish clergyman from succumbing to injuries identical
to those which had felled Bryant.

But the narrator's admonition that Casaubon's 'very *name* carried an
impressiveness hardly to be measured without a precise chronology of
scholarship' carries further connotations. On page 159 of her Notebook,
amidst quotations from Ovid and Spenser, George Eliot writes: 'Curious
to turn from Shakespeare to Isaac Casaubon, his contemporary.' In her
rereading of Renaissance works, she had obviously been struck by the
fact that Isaac Casaubon the theologian, considered to have been the
most erudite man of his age, was born five years before – and died two
years before – that upstart crow who had so 'little Latin and less Greek.'
By lending Casaubon's name to the weak-eyed and weak-legged husband
of Dorothea Brooke, George Eliot once again extracted meanings from
historical fact that she then metamorphosed into the fabric of her
fiction.

Isaac Casaubon was a Swiss scholar and linguist who had studied
Greek at Lausanne, the same city in which Dorothea Brooke as a schoolgirl meets M. Liret, the clergyman whom she regards as 'the most interesting man she had ever seen' until she encounters a new father-sub-
stitute in Mr Casaubon (2:13). (It also ought to be remembered that
Dorothea wants Mr Casaubon to 'teach her the languages' so that she
can read 'Latin and Greek aloud to [him], as Milton's daughters did to
their father' [7:47]). A Protestant, Isaac Casaubon was protected by
the Catholic convert Henry IV of France – a figure twice mentioned in
Middlemarch (once by the narrator who seizes on the inconsistency of
Mr Brooke's hopes that the fictional Casaubon might be made a bishop
and once by Mr Brooke himself as he visits Casaubon's estate).[23] Upon
the assassination of King Henri IV in 1610, Casaubon migrated to England, where he was welcomed by another royal patron, James, and
made prebendary of Canterbury and Westminster until his death in
1614.

Isaac's son Meric Casaubon (1599-1671), though equally learned
and just as productive, never wrote works as valuable as his father's.
Meric's *Treatise Concerning Enthusiasm* (1655), a markedly unenthu-
siastic, dry work that promises far more than it delivers, resembles the
productions of the fictional Mr Casaubon, who is described at one
point as being 'sensitive without being enthusiastic' (29:206); like the

'Parerga' by which Mr Casaubon claims to test his public's responses, Meric's *Treatise* is composed of fragments that never cohere into the intended grand opus of syncretic scholarship.

A 'precise chronology of scholarship' thus allows us to see the irony involved in the naming of the Reverend Edward Casaubon. Like his six-teenth- and seventeenth-century namesakes, Mr Casaubon is undeni-ably a man of 'profound learning' (1:8). But just as Meric Casaubon was, for all his erudition, far less original than his father, the contem-porary of Shakespeare, had been, so is this latter-day Casaubon a dis-tinct comedown from both Casaubon *père* and Casaubon *fils*. In chapter 29 the narrator of *Middlemarch* finally assesses Mr Casaubon. No longer relying on indirection,[24] he now indicts the author of the Key to all Mythologies for lacking both the 'ardour' and the 'energy' required for such an epic undertaking. It is noteworthy that the words 'ardour' and 'energy' are reserved in *Middlemarch* for Dorothea and Lydgate and are associated with the powers of imagination which the former learns to channel but the latter misuses. Moreover, the words are also associated with the entire *Zeitgeist* of the Renaissance, Reformation, and Counter-Reformation, an era of vision to which George Eliot had already turned in *Romola* and in *The Spanish Gypsy*. In *Middlemarch*, the Renaissance, an age of poetry and intensity, acts as an ironic backdrop for the pro-saic endeavours of the novel's main characters.

Mr Casaubon remains a parody of the 'compleat' Renaissance man. His naming is no more coincidental than the naming of Humphrey and Elinor Cadwallader, who bear the Christian names of a duke and duch-ess in *2 Henry VI*, or the naming of Bulstrode, who bears the name of Bulstrode Whitelocke the Puritan supporter of Cromwell who refused to impeach King Charles because he was 'too conscientious to do what he thought wrong,'[25] or the naming of the Reverend Camden Fare-brother, who bears the name of the erudite secularist who, though a clergyman, stressed an empirical explanation of history in his *Annals of the Age of Elizabeth*.[26] Still 'crawling,' in Ladislaw's words, 'after men of the last century,' men who were themselves crawling after the seminal minds of the century before them, Mr Casaubon belongs to the fag-end of the Enlightenment (22:164). The cosmology of the Renais-sance, as vibrant for Isaac Casaubon as it was for a Shakespeare or Milton, has, for him, become an antiquarian relic.

Casaubon is repeatedly associated with Milton through Dorothea's faulty idealization. And he resembles that Milton, who egotistically exploited the young women in his household. But only an 'unfavourable reflection' of Milton would render nothing more than this external 'facial angle' (10:62). Implicit in the comparison between the two men, there is also a contrast between Casaubon and that egotistically sublime imagination which relied on its Renaissance learning, on classical myth and biblical history, to create a new imaginative whole. Mr Casaubon is quite correct when he tries to remind Dorothea that Milton was a dispassionate husband and an unloving father who caused his daughters to rebel against him (7:47); yet this same Milton possessed the poetic passion that allowed him, in Coleridge's fine phrase, to attract 'all forms and things to himself in the unity of his own Ideal.'[27]

On several occasions in the novel, Mr Casaubon's 'frigid rhetoric' is pointedly compared to the professions of ardour and devotion of the Elizabethan sonneteers; in chapter 29, for example, the narrator undercuts Mr Casaubon's desire to 'eternize' himself through love and fame by calling attention to the disparity between past and present: 'he would neglect no arrangements for [Dorothea's] happiness: in return, he should receive family pleasures and leave behind him that copy of himself which seemed so urgently required of a man — to the sonneteers of the sixteenth century. Times had altered since then, and no sonneteer had insisted on Mr Casaubon's leaving a copy of himself; moreover, he had not yet succeeded in issuing copies of his mythological key.'[28] In a novel which employs the literature of the sixteenth and seventeenth centuries as a model for its own presentation of truth,[29] this allusion to the sonneteers who wrote during the days of Isaac Casaubon carries the same sort of covert irony as the allusion to 'sugared invention' made by Lydgate — that other character doomed by a defective imagination.

Like Lydgate the anatomist, Casaubon the historian is George Eliot's foil. And, once again, he is her foil because of an identity in their aims. In his first speech, Casaubon dolefully confesses that his mind 'is somewhat like the ghost of an ancient, wandering about the world and trying mentally to construct it as it used to be, in spite of ruin and confusing changes'(2:13). The statement reveals the attributes which lead Dorothea to link him with the poet Milton and which allow us, too, to detect a kinship between his aims and those of the narrator who, after Fielding's manner, assumes the guise of 'belated historian' writing an epic in prose (15:105). George Eliot the creator looks askance at Casaubon because she also wants to erect a structure that might protect her — and her readers — from meaninglessness and confusing changes. She chastises him, not for his failure to erect a rival structure, but for the meanness of his building materials. Casaubon's deficient powers of feeling prevent him from understanding what George Eliot states in her 'Notes on Form in Art,' namely, that poetry begins when 'passion weds thought by finding expression in an image' and that poetic form begins accordingly as the 'expression of emotional states.' As a literalist who tries to divest tradition of fable, Casaubon is a negative demonstration of George Eliot's claim, in her essay, that 'fiction or invention,' can be as true or truer to reality than 'ascertained external fact.' Casaubon is unaware that by rearranging and redistributing the fictions of other human minds he is himself a maker of fictions: 'But what is fiction other than an arrangement of events or feigned correspondences to pre-dominant feeling? We find what destiny pleases; we make what pleases us — or what we think will please others.'[30]

Casaubon tries to trace all human myths to a common source, an origin that can be anchored in history and thus become pinpointed, verifiable, ascertained as unfeigned external fact. Yet he fails to understand that history itself can be a fiction based on feeling. In his 'Defence of Poesy,' Sidney contends that 'a feigned example hath as much force to teach as a true example' and even more force to move us, 'since the feigned [example] may be turned to the highest key of passion.' To prove his point, Sidney cites examples wherein 'a poet and a historian concur' and alludes to Herodotus as well as to Xenophon's fiction of Cyrus.[31]

Casaubon, however, fails to recognize the common emotional basis that ought to bind the interests of historian and artist. Dorothea asks him whether *he* cares about the frescoes to which he professes to be willing to conduct her because 'most persons think it worth while to visit' works either 'designed or painted by Raphael.' He is caught off his guard: 'They are, I believe, highly esteemed. Some of them represent the fable of Cupid and Psyche, which is probably the romantic invention of a literary period, and cannot, I think, be reckoned as a genuine mythical product' (20:146). His measured answer superbly exemplifies his shortcomings. This classifier of myths is totally unmoved by myth itself. The allegorical and erotic implications of the same fable that attracted the neo-Hellenist painters of the end of the eighteenth-century and that drew Coleridge, Keats, and Pater to revive the myth of Psyche in the nineteenth century are of no interest to him. Apuleius and Ovid used the story of Psyche as an example of the powers of metamorphosis; Casaubon's literal mind cannot metamorphose the tale about the maiden who became divine. He must dismiss it as a fabrication, a 'romantic invention of some literary period.' The scholar who has already been metaphorically associated with underground passages, labyrinths, gloomy catacombs, and Mandeville's 'Land of Darknesse' ought at least to have remembered that the story of Cupid and Psyche was engraved on Roman sarcophagi to signify the transmigration of the soul. Had he so remembered, this clergyman who is so doubtful of an after-life might perhaps have desisted from trying to control Dorothea with his 'dead hand' from the grave.

It is his inability to see that 'feigned examples' have as much force to teach as factual ones which makes Casaubon, ironically described in chapter 3 as Milton's instructive Raphael, the 'affable archangel,' such a poor instructor for Dorothea: 'There is hardly any contact more depressing to a young ardent creature than that of a mind in which full years of knowledge seem to have issued in a blank absence of interest or sympathy' (20:146). Shortly before his death, Mr Casaubon tries to teach his young wife the meaning of the 'portents before the birth of Cyrus' that Herodotus describes in his *History*. But his impotent imagination has had its effects on Dorothea, who, by now, has ceased to be interested in either myth or history. Even poetry, 'the sacred chime of favourite hymns,' has become 'dreary' to a mind unaware of Mr Casaubon's impending death.

But if Dorothea does not care about Herodotus, the narrator of *Middlemarch,* who has already faulted Dorothea for her toy-box notions of history, does. George Eliot asserts that there is a relation between her aims as a novelist and those of the Father of History: 'much of the same sort of movement and mixture went on in old England as we find in older Herodotus, who also, in telling what *had been,* thought it well to take a woman's lot for his starting point' (11:71, italics added).

At first glance, the novelist-historian's identification with older Herodotus seems to be made with tongue in cheek; George Eliot's eight-book novel bears few resemblances to his nine-volume history. But the narrator, who so often in the course of the novel encourages us to use our 'power of comparison a little more effectively' (16:123), helps the reader's imagination by referring to Herodotus' story of Io. To expand his account of the events which culminated in the triumph of the Greeks over their Persian invaders into a more universal history of Asia Minor, Herodotus devised a framework not at all unlike George Eliot's own. Just as she retreats forty years in history to the Reform Bill era, so does he go back seventy years in order to trace the course of events from the rise of Cyrus to the defeat of Xerxes. At the same time, however, Herodotus impresses epic overtones on his historical account by straying into myth, the dawn of history, in the opening of his first book. To provide an archetype for the historical enmity between Greeks and non-Greeks, he relates the story of the abduction of Io, who, in the sardonic *Middlemarch* reference, 'as a maiden apparently beguiled by attractive merchandise, was the reverse of Miss Brooke, and in this respect perhaps bore more resemblance to Rosamond Vincy' (11:71). The analogy becomes clear: Herodotus the historiographer begins his account with fiction, the story of Io and the myths of the rape of Europa and Helena; George Eliot the novelist begins with the saga of the infant St Theresa as an historical archetype for her fiction. Feigned truth and historical truth coalesce, blended by the passion of feeling which Sidney, in the quotation recorded in George Eliot's Note-book calls, 'the sweet food of sweetly uttered knowledge.'[32] As Sidney states in his 'Defence,' 'historiographers ... have been glad to borrow of poets. So Herodotus entitled his history by the name of the nine Muses; and both he and all the rest that followed him either stole or usurped of poetry their passionate describing of passions.'[33]

III

In her 'Notes on Form in Art,' George Eliot declares that 'Form begins in the choice of rhythms and images as signs of a mental state.' I have looked at some of the 'rhythms' created through the fabric of allusion that operates in *Middlemarch*. And I have chosen to focus on allusions

related to the characters of Lydgate and Casaubon, because the novelist
subordinates the notions of reality of these two characters to that view
of form which prevails in the novel of which they are a part. The fixity
of Lydgate's and Casaubon's structures are at odds with the fluidity of
the rhythms and images created by George Eliot. The novelist broadens
the basis of our understanding — and constantly heightens our pleasure
— by allowing us to discover connections unperceived by the characters,
who remain limited by the conditions under which they labour. Gradually, the reader becomes trained to see universal 'wholes' where the
characters see only particulars. Yet not only the vision of the characters
comes under George Eliot's scrutiny. In the first paragraph of chapter
19, the chapter which introduces us to Dorothea's Roman honeymoon,
we are told:

In those days the world in general was more ignorant of good and evil
by forty years than it is at present. Travellers did not often carry full
information on Christian art either in their heads or in their pockets;
and even the most brilliant English critic of the day mistook the flower-
flushed tomb of the ascended Virgin for an ornamental vase due to the
painter's fancy. Romanticism, which has helped to fill some dull blanks
with love and knowledge, had not yet penetrated the times with its
leaven and entered everybody's food.

Again, a cryptic allusion must be closely examined before its full
meaning can be understood and its relation to other images and
rhythms be appreciated. The brilliant critic of the day referred to is
William Hazlitt. In his book, *A Journey Through France and Italy*
(1826), Hazlitt assumed that the 'Popish' representations of the Virgin
Mary were little more than a 'transposition of the Pagan Mythology' of
Greek and Roman 'superstitions.' George Eliot corrects Hazlitt's anti-
Catholic bias by showing that his statement is based on the mistaken
supposition that the 'flowers and the urn' so often depicted in paintings
of the Assumption are identical to the offerings to Flora and Ceres depicted in pagan art. His lapse is quickly explained: insufficiently aware
of Christian iconographic tradition, too provincial to have sampled a
sufficient number of representations of the ascending Virgin, Hazlitt
failed to realize that the flowered urn in the foreground of paintings

such as Filipino Lippi's is but a stylized version of the full-flowered sarcophagus found in more realistic representations of the Assumption.

But why is this pedantic emendation brought up by the narrator at this particular point in the novel? Why is a lack of 'information about Christian art' paired with the ironic assertion that, forty years ago, the world was 'more ignorant of good and evil'? Let us first look at what comes immediately before the passage from chapter 19 that I have cited. Chapter 18 ends with a conversation between Mr Farebrother and Lydgate. Emulating the words of Mr Tulliver in *The Mill on the Floss*, Mr Farebrother first laments, 'The world has been too strong for *me*, I know.' He then adds, 'But then I am not a mighty man — I shall never be a man of renown. The choice of Hercules is a pretty fable; but Prodicus makes it easy work for the hero, as if the first resolves were enough. Another story says that he came to hold the distaff, and at last wore the Nessus shirt.' In depreciating his weaknesses Mr Farebrother distinguishes between two variant myths about the mighty Hercules. As narrated by the Sophist Prodicus, Hercules seems a grand and heroic figure because he has an absolute freedom of choice. As suggested by other accounts, however, Hercules seems puny, denigrated by his sub- mission to Deianeira. Farebrother applies the latter parable to himself, although he is — and will remain — a single man. It will, however, be- come applicable to his interlocutor. Lydgate, the masculine hero of this novel without a hero, scorns Farebrother for his failings and tends to think of himself rather complacently as that 'mighty man' soon to gain a 'renown' that Farebrother admits he will never attain. But Lydgate does not yet know that marriage will be as fatal to him as to Hercules and that he will be forced to wear the Nessus shirt given to him by a new Deianeira.

If we now move from the end of chapter 18 to the description that opens chapter 19, we are invited to view first 'the reclining Ariadne, then called the Cleopatra' in the 'marble voluptuousness of her beauty' and, subsequently, 'another figure standing against a pedestal, whose form, not shamed by the Ariadne, was clad in Quakerish grey drapery' (19:140). Here, too, myth is adapted so that it can yield new meanings. Just as there are two variants of the Hercules myth, so are there two variants of the story of Hercules' admirer and emulator, Theseus, and of his relationship to Ariadne. George Eliot had already used the

Theseus and Ariadne story in *Romola*. In the Homeric version which
was followed by Ruskin in his *Fors Clavigera* — a work which, by the
way, appeared in instalments at the same time as *Middlemarch* —
Theseus is innocent of Ariadne's death; in the version of Plutarch which
George Eliot consulted Theseus is responsible for deserting Ariadne on
the island of Naxos.

Let us now try to thread through a few of the patterns created
through that 'process of grouping or association' to which George Eliot
refers in her 'Notes on Form in Art.' The allusions to Hercules and his
Nessus shirt, to Cleopatra, and to Ariadne refer to fictions about victims
betrayed by a member of the opposite sex. If Lydgate is a Hercules or
an Antony betrayed by his uxoriousness, Dorothea is an Ariadne betrayed by a man — by the sallow *Geistlicher* whom Adolf Neumann
immediately confuses with 'her father.' The epigraph to chapter nineteen ratifies this interpretation: L'altra vedete ch'ha fatto alla guanca /
Della sua palma, sospirando, letto' ('The other see, who, sighing, has
made a bed for her cheek with the palm of her hand'). The quotation is
taken from Dante's *Purgatory* and refers to still another victim, Charles
Valois, a son sacrificed by the excessive ambitions of his father, Philip III
of France. The change from Dante's masculine 'l'altro' to the feminine
'l'altra' is deliberate. We are meant to read in Charles' plight the suffering of Dorothea, another innocent confronting experience. In chapter
20, she, too, will be sobbing bitterly.

There are complications, however, which prevent us from seeing
Dorothea as exclusively a victim of treachery. Can Mr Casaubon really
be identified — as is Tito Melema in *Romola* — with the treacherous
young Theseus? Ought he not rather, as the images of labyrinths associated with him suggest, be identified with the Minotaur? And, if so, is
Ladislaw then to be seen as a Theseus who will deliver a new Ariadne
from a mythical monster? The fact that two alternate versions of the
myth exist, like the fact that the statue of the Ariadne is not yet known
as such to the tourists, prevents the reader from succumbing to any
such straightforward allegorization. If Dorothea is an Ariadne who was
never betrayed by Theseus, yet victimized nonetheless by fate, perhaps
it is her own confusion which led her to see a delivering Theseus in a
Minotaur that is to blame for her present predicament. The question of
free will, raised by the Hercules myth, thus is raised again. But no answer

needs to be given. Ladislaw's contention in chapter 22 that Dorothea
has received a faulty education by being brought to embrace 'some of
these horrible notions that choose the sweetest women to devour — like
Minotaurs,' would place the blame on neither Casaubon nor Dorothea
but on those same 'conditions of an imperfect social state' at which
George Eliot herself lashes out in her Finale.

The allusions to Hercules, Dante, Cleopatra, and Ariadne thus com-
plicate our responses to the literal fabric of the narrative. Taken together, they yoke the about-to-be-told story of Dorothea's unhappiness
as a married woman to the still-deferred story of Lydgate's marriage to
Rosamond. In addition, they alert us to the symbolic mode of behold-
ing reality of a Naumann who sees 'Mistress Second-Cousin as antique
form animated by Christian sentiment — a sort of Christian Antigone'
and of a Will Ladislaw who, though less interested in the painter's
Plastik, responds similarly to Dorothea. It is Will who now realizes that
Dorothea is not 'coldly clever' but 'adorably simple and full of feeling.'
His imagination allows Dorothea to rise above the ruins of classical and
Christian art to which she has been brought by her dead and deadening
husband. On meeting Dorothea for the second time in his life, Ladislaw
canonizes her into the saint with a 'heart large enough for the Virgin
Mary' that Tertius Lydgate will not come to recognize until near the
end of his travails (76:563).

It is in Rome, the 'city of visible history' that Ladislaw, that un-
formed Romantic conscience, signifies his love for Dorothea by calling
her the best part of a poet — 'a poem.' Dorothea must be brought to
Rome so that she can reject Mr Casaubon's sterile notions of reality.
The pieces that Casaubon vainly tries to combine now stare at her in all
their 'fragmentariness'; they remain unintegrated disparates: 'all that
was living and warm-blooded seemed sunk in the deep degeneracy of a
superstition divorced from reverence' (20:143). By seeing only such a
sundering, Dorothea sees what Hazlitt, that other Protestant visitor,
perceived. In her innocence, she does not know that she, the Eve who
wanted instruction from a debased archangel, is also that second Eve
who brought love into the world. She has thirsted for knowledge, for
the fruit of the forbidden tree, and yet she has, in her own person, all
along possessed the key to all mythologies. The world of inert fixities,
a universe of death, that spreads out before her eyes 'like a disease of

the retina' is still seen by her through Casaubon's eyes. But Will, whose
first name is that of Isaac Casaubon's eminent contemporary, possesses
the imagination required to thaw Casaubon's frozen landscape. Ladislaw
is able to communicate to Dorothea 'the enjoyment he got out of the
very miscellaneousness of Rome, which made the mind flexible with
constant comparison'; he saves her from seeing human history as but
'a set of box-like partitions without vital connection' (22:157). But it
is the narrator and the artist who speaks through him who can combine
Ladislaw's raw imagination with genuine knowledge. The narrator explains that the 'fragmentariness' that so depresses Dorothea could easily
have been avoided: 'To those who have looked at Rome with the quick-
ening power of a knowledge which breathes a growing soul into all
historic shapes, and traces out the suppressed transitions which unite
all contrasts, Rome may still be the spiritual centre and interpreter of
the world' (20:143).

Ladislaw is uninterested in literal 'sources' — be they of the Nile or
of mythology; he wants to preserve some 'unknown regions' as 'grounds
for the poetic imagination' (9:60).[35] For this sense, he is favourably
contrasted to those misusers of knowledge, Lydgate and Casaubon. For
all his imagination, however, Ladislaw lacks the supplementary knowledge and experience necessary for the formation of great art. 'You leave
out the poems,' says Dorothea to him, 'I think they are wanted to complete the poet' (22:166). She is right. Although she becomes his 'poem,'
he remains subordinate to her. It is the novelist and not Ladislaw who
can capture Dorothea's voice — 'the voice of a soul' that becomes so
incalculably diffusive.

And so we are left with Dorothea herself, a seeker who must renounce her quest for knowledge, a voice whose language remains simple
and unadorned. She incarnates the 'idealistic in the real' and as such
epitomizes the view of form adopted in the novel built around her. The
opening paragraph of chapter 1 should not be taken lightly: 'Miss Brooke
had the kind of beauty which seems to be thrown into relief by poor
dress. Her hand and wrist were so finely formed that she could wear
sleeves not less bare of style than those in which the Blessed Virgin
appeared to Italian painters.'

We can now return to chapter 19. If it locates Dorothea in a necro-
polis, a city of tombs to which she has been taken by her musty

husband, it also marks for us the point of her ascension in the novel. Like Maggie Tulliver at St Ogg's or Romola at Florence, Dorothea is forced to suffer in the City of Experience, forced to admit the imperfection of the constructs which she — like Lydgate and Casaubon — has tried to impose on the external world. To eyes which unduly magnified Casaubon and his aims, Rome must present a vision of nothingness; to such eyes, there can be no unity amidst its shards. But in Rome Dorothea also learns instinctively what Ladislaw the namer tries to put into hyperbolic words. Only the power of feeling can animate human life. And so, at the same time that she is brought to realize the futility of Casaubon's endeavours and the sterility of their marriage, her pity for this petty and unhappy man mounts and mounts. Innocent yet experienced, virginal yet maternal, she becomes like the Mother of Mercy. Her capacity for pity soothes Casaubon's last days; that same capacity later gains her a new convert in Lydgate, Casaubon's fellow rationalist. It is this pity also that makes Ladislaw finally admit his dependency on his best poem: ' "You teach me better," said Will ... There was a gentleness in his tone which came from the unutterable contentment of perceiving — what Dorothea was hardly conscious of — that she was travelling into the remoteness of pure pity and loyalty towards her husband' (37:269).

In chapter 19, the narrator of *Middlemarch* corrects Hazlitt, not out of scholarly scrupulosity, but because that so brilliant critic was unable to see a greater universality in the flower-flushed tomb of the ascended Virgin. The narrator praises Romanticism, in the next sentence, not only for its 'knowledge' — a knowledge which Hazlitt should have possessed before yoking 'Popish' representations to their presumed pagan counterparts — but also for its 'love.' The same attitude informs the other examples I have cited. Whether the myth of Cupid and Psyche is 'the romantic invention of a literary period,' as Mr Casaubon asserts, or not, what truly matters is its universal essence. Hazlitt should have seen that emotional essences can bind Christian and pagan art, that the dogmas of all religions have a common source in the ageless questions of 'good and evil.' Whether the reclining Ariadne is known as Cleopatra or by her true name, does not matter. The statue's 'voluptuousness' does make for the same 'fine bit of antithesis' that Naumann the artist is quick to spot (19:140). That antithesis becomes enfleshed when, much later in the novel, an Ariadne wronged by Ladislaw nonetheless embraces and comforts her rival, Lydgate's voluptuous Cleopatra. The two women are united through the power of feeling. Again, whether this or that myth of Hercules or Theseus is employed, all myths, like history, are nothing more than the record of some very basic and simple human emotions. To change Dante's historical Charles of Valois into a fictitious Dorothea Brooke is therefore no sleight of hand: there are emotions that remain archetypal, despite the differences between men and women.

Thus it is that an 'ingenious pattern-work' which, like a Beethoven symphony, relies on the confluence of hundreds of smaller tributary motifs and movements, should nonetheless depend on the same earthly Madonna, the same creed of feeling, presented in George Eliot's earlier fictions. In a novel where 'tricks with vocables take the place of living words,' feeling remains a non-verbal state. Asked by Celia to describe the story of her infatuation with Ladislaw, Dorothea refuses: 'No, dear, you would have to feel with me, else you would never know' (84:602).

IV

The reader of *Middlemarch* is asked to feel with Dorothea. She is, as everybody acknowledges, the major, the most memorable, character in the novel. Dorothea is not even brought in contact with that other projection of Mary Ann Evans, the homely Mary Garth, a duckling who does not turn into a swan, who stays in the provinces, who is loyal to a father, who accepts the world's limitations, who has no epic pretensions to give up. Still, Dorothea is implicitly likened to Mary when she, too, reclaims an aimless young man and settles for motherhood. The court-ships of both Will and Dorothea and Fred and Mary are rendered through images of childhood which return us to that child-pilgrimage of a little girl walking hand-in-hand with her still smaller brother used as 'a fit beginning' in the proem which George Eliot called Prelude. In chapter 57, Fred takes a step closer to becoming a Garth when he joy-fully reports to Mary that her father 'treated me as if I were his son.' That chapter, interestingly enough, is headed by a sonnet about chil-dren living in a make-believe world of love and faith created for them by Sir Walter Scott. The sonnet is George Eliot's own. Very likely it is

one of those 'Brother and Sister' sonnets which George Eliot finished in
July of 1869, a few days before beginning the ur-*Middlemarch*.

'I made a poem,' she wrote years later, 'in the form of eleven sonnets
after the Shakespeare type on the childhood of a brother and sister —
little descriptive bits on the mutual influences in their small lives. This
was always one of my best loved subjects.'[36] It is easy to see why a sonnet written as part of such a cycle might be deemed appropriate as an epigraph for the story of Fred and Mary, the childhood sweethearts whose
idyll softens the impact of the disappointments the other characters
have to suffer. But why should Dorothea so often be referred to as a
child in her relations with Ladislaw? The pair are described as 'two fond
children who were talking confidentially about birds' (39:287); even at
the height of their passion, when they are speechless, they stand 'with
their hands clasped, like two children, looking out on the storm'
(83:593).

In the sentence from 'Notes on Form in Art' that I quoted earlier,
George Eliot states that 'Form begins in the choice of rhythms and
images as signs of a *mental state.*' I do not know, nor do I think that
anybody can ever know, what 'mental state' originated the rhythms
and images of *Middlemarch*. The key to the novel's private mythologies
can never be found — it can at best remain a conjecture, and an uncertain one at that. Let me, however, venture one conjecture — less
about the state of mind that led George Eliot to write her novel, than
about an allusion which may have a possible bearing on a key to
Middlemarch.

I have documented the implications of names such as Lydgate and
Casaubon and shown their literary origins. But what about the name of
the girl who is likened to a fine quotation from 'one of our elder poets'?
Dorothea's last name is interwoven with the countless allusions to currents and streams — of water as well as of feeling and thought — which
recur throughout the novel; it is related to the metaphors of fishing,
fishes, and fish-gods; it is opposed to the metaphors of pools and lakes,
stagnant bodies of water, associated first with Casaubon and then with
Lydgate; it is fused with the multiple references to motion and movement and thus connected to the flow of history itself. But why
Dorothea Brooke?

In *The Prelude,* Wordsworth invokes the breezes and the streams of
his childhood so that, reanimated with feeling, he can again consecrate
himself to his vatic task; eager to animate his rhyme he identifies with
that Milton who invoked 'Siloa's Brook that flow'd, / Fast by the Oracle
of God.'[37] Yet, unlike his predecessor, Wordsworth cannot rely on visi-
tations by Urania to restore his faith in humanity and in the self.
Thrice, therefore, in the course of his poem, at its most climactic
points, does he invoke his sister:

> and then it was
> That the beloved Woman in whose sight
> Those days were pass'd, now speaking in a voice
> Of Sudden admonition, like a brook
> That does but cross a lonely road
> ...
> Maintain'd for me a saving intercourse
> With my true self.

The passage which likens Wordsworth's sister Dorothy to a 'brook' and
seizes on her 'voice' occurs in book X of the 1805 *Prelude,* in the verse
paragraph immediately before the poet's allusion to Timoleon.[38] Wordsworth credits his sister with preserving him 'still a Poet' and making him
seek his office upon earth, and nowhere else, so that by 'human love /
Assisted' he can be conducted through weary labyrinths into the light
of open day. Dorothea Brooke, whose Aeolian voice thrills Ladislaw the
poet and whose 'voice of deep-souled womanhood' is so long remembered by Lydgate, the man with a poet's name (58:433), may well have
found her name through George Eliot's reading of these very lines.

There is, indeed, some other support for my conjecture. Earlier in
The Prelude, Wordsworth recreates his first encounter with Dorothy;
remembering Coleridge's own pun on her name, 'our sister gift-of-
god,' he calls her his 'sole Sister,' 'Thy Treasure also,' a 'gift then first
bestow'd.'[39] He places his first meeting with his sister on the 'gentle
Banks' of the river Emont, 'hitherto unnam'd in Song,' and speculates
that the same spot might have been visited by another brother and
sister in the days of Queen Elizabeth — by Sir Philip Sidney and Mary,

Countess of Pembroke. Going a step further, Wordsworth fancies that snatches of the *Arcadia,* like his own poem, may well have been inspired on the same spot 'by fraternal love.' And yet Wordsworth places another woman on that scene, 'Another Maid there was, who also breath'd / A gladness o'er that season.'[40] That other woman was to become his wife, Mary. If one recalls the similar use of the Elizabethan age as a backdrop for poetic parallels in *Middlemarch* and remembers the use of Sidney's phrase, perhaps my conjecture can be seen to have some foundation in fact. Mary Garth in *Middlemarch* was originally called Mary Dove; it was at Dove Cottage where Wordsworth settled with the two women he credits for reviving his poetic soul. Last but not least, the *Life of Sidney* consulted by Wordsworth for the fictitious parallel he implants in his poem was written by Fulke Greville, Lord *Brooke.*

My conjecture may be itself a fiction. Critics, particularly those who study novels, are not immune to the tendency to fictionalize. But even if fictional, my conjecture nonetheless illustrates, I think, the truth of what I have been trying to demonstrate in this paper: the intricacies of the associations George Eliot created in the poem in prose called *Middlemarch.* We must not shy away from these intricacies if we want to retrace the operations of the creative imagination that built in *Middlemarch* a reality designed to demonstrate, what Lydgate's microscope could not, 'the more intimate relations of living structure.'

In her attempts to define men's thoughts after a truer order than Lydgate's, George Eliot created a new form — an epic that is not an epic, a history that is a fiction, a work of prose that can and must be read like a poem. Like the Spenser or Milton whom she reread and like the Wordsworth of *The Prelude* she loved and the Byron of *Don Juan* she admired but disliked, she was led to revitalize the old heroic myths by creating new forms. Like all poets, she had to resort to words to defend herself against the chaos of temporal disorder. Still, beneath that ultra-complicated verbal pattern-work that is *Middlemarch* lies a 'state of mind' quite as simple and pristine as that desire to resist 'the dire years whose awful name is Change' (sonnet XI) which George Eliot expressed in 1869 in the 'Brother and Sister' sonnets. The female speaker of those sonnets wishes to escape into the simplicity of an infantile world. She wants to return to the child's ignorance of disjunction, to a stage where the only not-self, the only contraries, exist in the 'loving difference of girl and boy' (sonnet IX).

Middlemarch is the product of a remarkable nineteenth-century mind — it is one of the most successful expressions of that encyclo-paedic desire to encompass the best that has been thought and felt for which that century is noted. Going beyond the mere perception of dis-parates, beyond a relativistic fragmentation of reality into unintegrated parts, the novel is a deeply mature work in which George Eliot has moved from *scientia* — knowledge — to *sophia,* wisdom. And yet, the novel's assimilating rhythms and images hide the same bald utterance that concludes the 'Brother and Sister' sonnets: 'But were another childhood-world my share / I would be born a little sister there' (sonnet XI). That utterance required a far more formidable expression before it could be fully accommodated. An admission of such an ele-mentary yearning had to be presented through indirections such as those that I have tried to retrace. Only in that way could the emotions of this wonderful, deeply passionate woman be wrought into the coarser emotions of mankind. We have not altered in the century that has elapsed since the publication of *Middlemarch,* despite our greater sophistication in questions of good and evil. George Eliot knew that if the men and women who read a novel were to attain a keener vision of the true emotions that give shape to the fictions devised by another's mind, they could hardly bear it. That knowledge would be like hearing the grass grow and the squirrel's heart beat and we might die of the roar that lies on the other side of silence. And therefore, she created in *Middlemarch* a fiction about the need for fictions.

NOTES

1 *The George Eliot Letters* G.S. Haight ed (New Haven 1954-55) V 3. Hereafter GEL.
2 John Clark Pratt, A *Middlemarch* Miscellany: An Edition, with Introduction and Notes, of George Eliot's 1868-1871 Notebook (unpublished dissertation, Princeton 1965) 182. I am greatly indebted to Professor Pratt's most helpful introduction and meticulous annotations. Hereafter his edition of the 1868-71 Notebook is referred to as NBM.
3 GEL IV 490
4 In book X of the 1805 *Prelude,* after crediting his sister for returning him to his 'true self,' the poet signifies his freedom from the oppression of

contemporary history by turning to Coleridge, who 'now, / Among the basest
and the lowest fallen / Of all the race of men, dost make abode / Where Etna
looketh down on Syracuse, / The city of Timoleon!' (915, 946-50; p 203 in
Stephen Gill and Ernest de Selincourt eds, *The Prelude or Growth of A
Poet's Mind* [London 1970]). Wordsworth compares the degenerate state of
Sicily to its 'loftiest years' under Timoleon and laments that those early
ideals, so superior to those of the French Revolution, should have been forgotten by Timoleon's nineteenth-century country-men and by the world at
large (950-65). For George Eliot's possible familiarity with and use of the
verse paragraph that precedes this passage, see below.

5   Thomas Warton *The History of English Poetry* (London 1840) I ccvi (cited
by Pratt NBM xxx); George Grote *History of Greece* (London 1862) I 344
(cited by Pratt NBM 187)

6   NBM 19

7   NBM 14

8   Sir Philip Sidney *Defence of Poesy* Dorothy M. Macardle ed (New York
1966) 10

9   Francis Meres *Palladis Tamia, Wits Treasury; being the second part of Wits
Commonwealth,* in *Elizabethan Critical Essays* Gregory Smith ed (Oxford
1904) II 315-16

10   See *Middlemarch,* Finale and chapter 3, respectively.

11   See NBM 144, 301

12   Grote I 344 (cited by Pratt NBM 187)

13   'Notes on Form in Art,' *Essays of George Eliot* Thomas Pinney ed (London
1963) 433

14   The Quarry for *Middlemarch* contains a section on 'Microscopic Discovery:
Cell Theory'; only a few months before she began *Middlemarch,* George Eliot
and Lewes had visited the newly founded Institute of Pathology in Vienna
and had used the most powerful microscopic lens in existence at the time.
Still, like the Milton who uses his acquaintance with Galileo's 'Optic Glass'
to suggest the existence of essences 'which perhaps' the astronomer 'yet never
saw' (*Paradise Lost* I.288, III.587-90), so George Eliot employs her even
greater scientific preparation to suggest that 'Signs are small measurable
things, but interpretations are illimitable' (3:18). She scoffs at the 'scientific
certitude' with which men like Lydgate treat women (Prelude) and laughs at
Mr Brooke's imperfect state of 'scientific prediction' about his niece's character (4:30). She asserts that no lens or mirror has yet been devised to render
an accurate picture of intangibles: 'Even with a microscope directed on a
water-drop we find ourselves making interpretations which turn out to be
rather coarse.' Reducing reality into smaller components does not help:
'whereas under a weak lens you may seem to see a creature exhibiting an
active voracity into which other smaller creatures actively play as if they
were so many animated tax-pennies, a stronger lens reveals to you certain
tiniest hairlets which make vortices for these victims while the swallower
waits passively at the receipt of custom.' 'In this way metaphorically

speaking,' she turns her knowledge of science against the presumption of those scientists who fail to admit that they, too, are allegorists, makers of fictive models of reality (6:44).

15   References in this paragraph are as follows: 13:93; 15:110, 113, 114.

16   References in this paragraph are: 19, 152; 10:69; 9:59; 56:402; 37:268; 56:402.

17   Sidney 32-3

18   'Notes on Form in Art' 436

19   'The Language of the Novel: Imagery' in *Middlemarch: Critical Approaches to the Novel* Barbara Hardy ed (London 1967) 87-124

20   In ibid, 35

21   The sub-title of Bryant's *A New System or Analysis of Ancient Mythology*

22   Charles Knight *The English Cyclopaedia: A New Dictionary of Universal Knowledge: Biography* (London 1856) I 986, 987

23   See chapters 7 and 9, respectively.

24   For a more extended discussion of the manipulation of point of view in George Eliot's treatment of Mr Casaubon see my *Laughter and Despair: Readings in Ten Novels of the Victorian Era* (Berkeley 1971) 181-7.

25   See Knight VI 677

26   See NBM 50-1, where George Eliot quotes a passage from Lecky's *Morals* (I 214), the sources of which are credited by Lecky to William Camden. According to Knight, Camden — like Farebrother in the novel — 'never married' (V 47). In Knight, George Eliot would also have discovered that Camden was given the prebend of Ilfracombe, where she and Lewes spend such a delightful time finding natural specimens like those which the fictional Farebrother has collected (see GEL II 238-55).

27   *Biographia Literaria* chapter fifteen

28   See also 5:37 and 6:45 for further references to Elizabethan sonneteers.

29   In *Middlemarch* more than half of those chapter-epigraphs not written by George Eliot herself are taken from the literature of the sixteenth- and seventeenth-centuries; those penned by herself are cast in a Browningesque imitation of Elizabethan language. (George Eliot had, by the way, read *The Ring and the Book,* that compendium of multitudinousness, before she wrote *Middlemarch.*) For the best assessment of her epigraphs, see D.L. Higdon, 'George Eliot and the Art of the Epigraph' *Nineteenth-Century Fiction* 25 (September 1970) 127-51.

30   'Notes on Form in Art' 435, 434

31   Sidney 18

32   See footnote 11, above.

33   Sidney 3-4

34   'Notes on Form in Art' 435

35   See the entry on page 123 of NBM: 'Alexander finding crocodiles in Ganges supposed he had found the head of the Nile — the premise being that crocodiles were only found in the Nile.'

36   To John Blackwood, 21 April 1873, GEL V 403

37   *Paradise Lost* I.11-12
38   *The Prelude* X.907-16; see footnote 4, above.
39   Ibid VI.214, 215, 218
40   Ibid VI.218-19, 225, 233-34

DAVID CARROLL

Middlemarch and
the externality of fact

Three phrases from George Eliot's novels will suggest the kind of idea I
wish to discuss in *Middlemarch*. The first comes from *Daniel Deronda*
and refers to 'the pressure of that hard unaccommodating Actual which
has never consulted our taste'; the second from the last page of *Middlemarch* admits that 'there is no creature whose inward being is so strong
that it is not greatly determined by what lies outside it'; and the third,
from which I take my title, comes from *The Mill on the Floss* and describes the failure of one of Mr Tulliver's plans, not, says George Eliot,
because his 'will was feeble, but because external fact was stronger.'
These phrases stress the existence of a reality which is out there, separate from the self, unmodifiable by our wishes; they convey a feeling
which is an integral part of the reading of any of George Eliot's novels.
This is the basis of her tough-minded, critical realism, the reason why
she attacks so many fictional conventions which pretend that the actual
is not unaccommodating, that the inner and the outer correspond, that
appearance is reality, and that character – in the words of that doubtful
aphorism – is destiny. All this ignores the truth that out there are the
external facts and circumstances, either as solid as the ruins and basili-
cas of Rome, or as subtle and intangible as the web of Middlemarch
gossip which spins itself through the novel. This is the fallen world of
George Eliot's fiction in which the link between desire and fulfilment
has been broken. Its opposite – the Eden world of childhood before
self-consciousness isolates the individual – is described most movingly

in *The Mill on the Floss*. That is the world 'where objects become dear to us before we had known the labour of choice, and where the outer world seemed only an extension of our own personality' (II 1:234). Time and place have not yet come into existence and so choice, with its inevitable deprivations, is not demanded from us. But when this identification of the self and the outer world is lost, then one is faced with the terrible ambiguity that reality is *both* inner and outer, and where one ends and the other begins is not at all clear. This is the moment of panic when the individual commits himself prematurely to one of two extreme oversimplifications. Either he disengages the mind and says that reality is there in the material world, or he insists that reality without mind is impossible for reality is a creation of the mind. You can either be a philosophical realist or a philosophical idealist. Or, if you prefer, you can be a Dodson or Tulliver: you can maintain that the mill on the river Floss is either a piece of property with a five per cent mortgage or you can see it as the embodiment of your emotional life. But you can't accept — what unfortunately it is — both simultaneously. The idea of the mind twisting and turning to escape this ambiguity, the 'twofold aspect' as George Henry Lewes called it, is a subject central to the novels. In *Middlemarch*, the contrasted research of Lydgate and Casaubon is emblematic of the materialist and idealist positions pushed to their extreme. Lydgate is examining the physical structure of the body and hopes to find in its inmost tissue — mind; Casaubon, on the other hand, is examining the constructs of men's thoughts, their myths, and he deduces that they will lead him out of mind to a reality which was in the first place — revealed. Each position seeks to become unitary by annexing the adjacent world of mind or matter and so escaping, without resolving, the ambiguity I have described.

The question I wish to ask about *Middlemarch* is how does George Eliot suggest that her characters should deal with external fact? The novel frames its answer in terms of perception — usually it is question of *seeing* in George Eliot — and frequently of scientific perception. The use, from the very first sentence of the novel, of scientific analogy and metaphor, those 'scientific conceits' which disturbed several of the contemporary reviewers (one saw them as a form of 'intellectual slang'), is clearly an attempt by George Eliot to get away from those fictional devices which blur the relation between inner and outer. The scientific analogies give a hard-edged clarity to the statement of the problem. Here is the mind, out there is something which is not mind. How do they come together? I intend first to distinguish three different modes of perception, and then to try to interpret with their help some of the human relationships in the novel.

The first piece of advice she gives – and this may seem more than obvious – is that one should look closely and carefully at the facts in whatever form they appear. George Eliot repeatedly exhorts her readers and characters to do this. The phrase that comes to mind is the one used by Ladislaw, the 'sturdy neutral delight in things as they were' (30:215). The adjective 'neutral' separates the delight from the mind's desires and wish-fulfilments. This ability to look carefully and objectively, the 'distinct appreciation of the value of evidence' George Eliot found so lacking in Dr Cumming, is, she insists, a moral quality. And in *Middlemarch* the activity of looking closely is constantly before us. Living seems to resolve itself at times into a pair of eyes getting closer and closer to an object, and when the eyes fail, instruments of illumination and magnification are used. This movement of focusing ever more minutely on an object of scrutiny can be seen in George Eliot's examination of Mrs Cadwallader's mysterious activities. 'Was there any ingenious plot, any hide-and-seek course of action,' asks the narrator, 'which might be detected by a careful telescopic watch? Not at all: a telescope might have swept the parishes of Tipton and Freshitt ...' (6:44) without discovering anything. We need to get closer to the facts than this. So we switch from the telescope to the microscope and to the rather ungainly scientific analogy: 'Even with a microscope directed on a water-drop we find ourselves making interpretations which turn out to be rather coarse'; you can easily, she says, mistake an active creature for a passive one and *vice versa*. What is needed is a 'stronger lens.' Then the very terms active and passive become irrelevant for now you discover, between the two creatures, the hidden medium which controls their relation. The same kind of movement occurs in George Eliot's account of the study of pathology at the time of the novel. Bichat's discovery was like 'the turning of gas-light ... on a dim, oil-lit street, showing new connections' (15:110). Lydgate's development of this thesis 'would be another light, as of oxy-hydrogen, showing the very grain of things ...' From oil-light, to gas-light, to oxy-hydrogen –

and finally back to Lydgate crouched over his microscope, looking for the living tissue of reality.

But scrutinizing the evidence carefully is only a beginning. Facts by themselves are not enough. You need to know how to look at them. They become meaningless and terrifying if allowed to thrust themselves without mediation upon the mind, as Dorothea discovers amid the insistent fragmentariness of Rome. Here, the disenchanted mind in its blank passivity is helplessly open to the irredeemable facts which force themselves upon it. Then the facts by their very isolation mislead, pervert, and destroy. There is no character in *Middlemarch* with quite the same commitment to the empirical reality of what he can see and touch as Tom Tulliver. Believed in to this extent, facts begin to kill and Maggie dies redeeming them with meaning. This kind of mind refuses to engage itself with the facts and so they come to it inexplicably, fragmented, and with disturbing force from out there. They constitute a proof that cannot be argued with. The throw of the dice can be seen as the most factual of all evidence because it is most immune to the mind's meddling. In this way facts turn into their opposite and become miracles.

To escape from the dead hand of fact and its perversions the mind needs to go beyond them and formulate a hypothesis. This brings us to our second mode of perception. When an hypothesis based upon probabilities is tested against the facts in order to substantiate and modify itself, we see the mutual interaction of inner and outer across the void that separates them. This explains why Ladislaw's reaction to Rome is so different from Dorothea's. Since he can supply 'the suppressed transitions which unite all contrasts,' the 'fragments [stimulate] his imagination and [make] him constructive' (22:157). The dead fragments are given 'vital connection' and revivified. The mind gives meaning, the external world gives substance. This is the interplay which excites George Eliot; then her prose quickens and irony is eschewed. Lydgate's researches show the mind at such a moment of fulfilment as it interacts creatively with the external world. If there are any purple patches in *Middlemarch,* this account of Lydgate's method of inquiry is certainly one of them. It begins characteristically with a dismissal of the traditional idea of the imagination — that activity of the *littérateur* who fabricates in words (those facile creations of the mind) a fanciful world from inside his own head. In contrast, Lydgate has chosen to engage *his* mind with a reality external to it. His is 'that arduous invention which is the very eye of research, provisionally framing its object and correcting it to more and more exactness of relation' (16:122). The mind is active and passive in turn, constructive and receptive in perfect mutuality with the outer world. This is disciplined invention, the work of 'the imagination that reveals subtle actions inaccessible by any sort of lens, but tracked in that outer darkness through long pathways of necessary sequence by the inward light which is the last refinement of Energy, capable of bathing even the ethereal atoms in its ideally illuminated space (16:122). It is noticeable that the mind brings its own light to the outer darkness and, most vividly, *bathes* the atoms in illumination and meaning. Lydgate is pursuing the interaction of mind and matter to the apotheosis – the discovery of mind in matter – where their separateness will be resolved and paradise will eventually be regained.

In descriptions of this kind George Eliot is very careful to retain the precise balance between the inner and outer reality. She is equally severe on the fanciful mind which getting out of control seeks to prescribe rather than describe reality, and on the mind which refuses to make the act of faith ahead of the facts. These two failings are dramatised amusingly and shrewdly in the opening chapters of the novel in the relationship between Dorothea and Celia. Dorothea has all the hypotheses and theory and sees only Mr Casaubon's soul; Celia has all the ungarnished facts and sees only the moles on his nose. The two connected parts of genuine investigation have become separated. One mind won't descend to commonplace detail, the other won't rise to a hypothesis. They quarrel and make up their quarrel, and then they quarrel again. And Mr Brooke, their uncle, reiterates their disagreements in his own mental oscillations. Whatever theory he may formulate to explain things, he can just as quickly demolish by adducing facts which contradict it. We see him, for example, informing the baffled Casaubon 'that the Reformation either meant something or it did not, that he himself was a Protestant to the core, but that Catholicism was a fact' (2:14). Even the theory that theory is a good thing has to be modified by the fact that it can be taken too far: 'I pulled up; I pulled up in time.' This again is clearly a rather radical idea which needs modifying in turn: 'But not too hard. I have always been in favour of a little theory: we must have Thought; else we shall be landed back in the dark ages' (2:13). The dialectic which keeps getting stuck in this way does give Brooke a humane awareness of what he calls 'the oddity of things.'

There is one final step – and this is the third mode of perception – in which the mind goes over the edge, as it were, in its own self-aggrandisement and seeks to prescribe the reality it is examining. Here mutual action and interaction is denied. By a unilateral act of will the mind insists that the outer world is an extension of itself. One might say that this, the sight of an hypothesis resisting contrary evidence, is for George Eliot the epitome of stupidity and pride. Casaubon's research on his Key to all Mythologies shows the intellect refusing to modify a hypothesis and so turning it into a deduction which determines its findings beforehand. He has 'undertaken to show that all the mythical systems ... were corruptions of a tradition originally revealed' (3:18). Once the mind has 'taken a firm footing there' in this deduction, then everything becomes 'intelligible, nay luminous.' Now it is simply a question of 'gathering in the great harvest of truth.' Gone is the fine equipoise between theory and fact as they influence each other. Instead of the mind bathing the facts in meaning, it insinuates itself around their spurious counterparts trying to avoid contact. Casaubon's theory 'floats among' the dead fragments of knowledge like embalming fluid.

The mind in the grip of a presupposition acts in a variety of ways in *Middlemarch*, the spectrum ranges from stupidity to villainy and – this is one of the corollaries of George Eliot's controlling scientific analogies – the one usually leads to the other. But she is tolerant of most of these variations for she knows that the mind in its own defence must create a theory by which to mediate with the outer world. And the difference between a creative hypothesis and self-willed presupposition may in the first instance be slight. But what she demands is that we become sensitive to the exact point where the mind meets the outer world, where the hypothesis comes into contact with the facts it is trying to explain, where the deduction begins to mould the evidence, where for example, Mrs Cadwallader's caustic tongue and sharp epigrams begin cutting reality into the shape she desires. This is the crucial area of interaction. In one sense, this *is* the reality of the novels – not the mind, not the external – but their meeting place. This is what

George Eliot means when she refers repeatedly to the 'medium' of Middlemarch society. It is the combination of all those intermingled webs spun between the mind and the external world, and, in the absence of any coherent social faith and order, it determines subtly and firmly the way in which life is interpreted and whether individuals are sacrificed or redeemed.

With the help of these definitions I wish now to examine two important human relations in the novel. One of these shows the mind on the rampage, the other demonstrates its disciplined working. But before I insinuate my hypothesis among the facts of the fiction one point needs to be made. I have been looking mainly at the use George Eliot makes of scientific analogies to clarify the relation between inner and outer; this is an essential part of her pragmatism. When, however, we switch our attention to the personal relations in the novel, an important new element appears. The scientific concepts assume that the reality being examined by the mind is inert, or at any rate, mindless; we are never told how the primitive tissue felt about Lydgate's inspired probings. But in human relations, mind acts and reacts upon mind, and the external facts are forming their own hypotheses. This complicates the application of the scientific analogies, but it is nevertheless surprising how far George Eliot is prepared to apply them to the human complexities of the novel.

Bulstrode, in order to satisfy his intense appetite for power and respectability, has formulated the hypothesis that he has been chosen by God as his special agent in the world. The influence he exercises within his dissenting sect, however, seems to him inadequate when he comes into contact with the world of business and commerce. The 'moment of transition,' as it is called, arrives when he is invited to become the 'confidential accountant' of Dunkirk's wealthy pawnbroking business. Now the hypothesis has to be tested against the facts. Can the Protestant ethic and the spirit of capitalism be reconciled in the relation between Bulstrode's 'sacred accountableness' to his God and his 'confidential accountancy' in business? He experiences 'moments of shrinking' as the unsavoury facts touch his delicate hypothesis, but the demands of the ego are too strong and Bulstrode allows the hypothesis — now hardening into a deduction — to rearrange things to suit his purposes. The rearrangement takes the form of his doctrine of instrumentality which is really a bargain he makes with his God. ' "I am sinful and nought – a vessel to be consecrated by use – but use me!" had been the mould into which he had constrained his immense need of being something important and predominating' (61:453). The terms are simple: you use me and I'll use you. It is a mutual exploitation. Now that the hypothesis has glossed over certain unpleasant facts, it is essential that it remain unquestioned, or else the demands of the self – what the self has become – will have to be revised. And so when Bulstrode's instrumentality is later threatened by the discovery of Dunkirk's daughter, just as he is about to marry the business-man's wealthy widow, he is forced to tamper with the evidence, suppress the facts, in order to keep his theory watertight. When the novel opens, the world seems to have arranged itself very much for Bulstrode's convenience, but of course, certain facts have been wilfully excluded from the scheme of things. They come roaring back in the shape of Raffles.

Raffles was the agent who discovered Dunkirk's runaway daughter; he had to be bribed and sent off with the unaccommodating facts to America. He was used, disposed of, and forgotten. This is the moral stupidity at the centre of Bulstrode's scheme of things; unlike the genuinely perceiving mind, active and passive in turn, Bulstrode is always active and his instruments always passive. But Raffles is more than an instrument; he has a rather unsavoury 'centre of self' of his own – made the more unsavoury by Bulstrode – which dares to see the banker as subordinate to his own plans. As soon as this is glimpsed, the very qualities which made this garrulous, superannuated Adonis of the bar-parlours such an excellent agent turn him instantly into the most frightening threat to Bulstrode's respectability. Apparently passive in Bulstrode's scheme of things, he is inevitably active in his own. He was, in the words of the novel, 'paid for keeping silence and carrying himself away' (61:452); this is no life for a man with ambitions of his own, and so now the terms of his disappearance are exactly reversed. He comes back talking compulsively and blackmailing his briber. It is almost as if the unpleasant facts have taken on a life of their own. Everything which Bulstrode has tried to gloss over – the plot to defraud, the shady foundations of his wealth, the whole disreputable world just beneath the respectable surface – come back demanding attention on that lovely summer evening when he is standing in his garden at Stone Court (53). The

speck interfering with his vision has turned into the very obstreperous
Raffles. This sudden independent life of his agent is completely inexplicable to Bulstrode — this is the moment of shock we come to recognize
in the novel: 'as if by some hideous magic, this loud, red figure had
risen before him in unmanageable solidity.' It is the switch from the
passive to the active voice. The man who was bribed now knows how to
blackmail; the man paid to keep silent now threatens to talk; the agent
who ferreted out Sarah Dunkirk now tracks down Bulstrode; and, most
significantly, the man used to buttress the banker's scheme of things
now comes back to exploit its weaknesses and demand his share of the
money. The symmetry of the situation is an excellent example of the
nemesis of human relations in the novel. Bulstrode has controlled his
agent by bribing him to carry out a certain task, channelling their relation entirely in this one direction; when the agent becomes active in his
own right the only channel open to him is the one laid down for him by
his employer and exploiter. He must for his own survival strike back
along this channel. This is why to the alarmed eyes of Bulstrode Raffles
has betrayed him by turning into his opposite; the man who was prepared to be bribed is now blackmailing. (You use me, and I'll use you.)
There is some pathos in Raffles' obstreperousness. A person denied an
independent existence is trying to gain recognition and the only way he
can do so is by asserting actively those sleazy qualities which made him
an instrument in the first place. He needs to be accepted: 'I should do
you credit among the nobs here,' he tells Bulstrode.

Bulstrode's 'usual paleness [has] ... taken an almost deathly hue' by
this time, for he knows that his whole scheme of things, his very character, is threatened by this florid figure. He knows he must regain control,
and so he desperately tries to recover some hold over his agent and
accomplice. But Raffles won't be pinned down again. Where does he
live? 'I have no particular attachment to any spot: I would as soon settle
hereabout as anywhere.' What is his job? 'I don't care about working
any more, what I want is an independence.' Bulstrode realizes that this
is what he will have to give him — the passive agent is successfully
blackmailing himself into an independent existence — but as he agrees
to pay him an annuity, Bulstrode desperately tries to cancel its implications. Much to Raffles' amusement, he tells him that if he
reappears in Middlemarch, 'I shall decline to know you.' Raffles

assures him, 'I should never decline to know you.' Later events
prove him wrong.

It is the perfectly complementary nature of the two men which is so
brilliantly handled by George Eliot. Not only in their appearance and
way of life, but also in their beliefs. The reason why Raffles offsets Bulstrode so perfectly is that he completes him. He is the missing element
which has made Bulstrode's deductive theory workable for so long. The
more Raffles is reminded of this by Bulstrode's decorous and pious respectability, the more he *must* seek to undermine it by ridicule. He
himself is a religious sceptic — 'no man felt his intellect so superior to
religious cant' — because Bulstrode has shown him the spurious quality
of his own belief. This is why Raffles' bad jokes are so coarse a parody.
'Still in the Dissenting line, eh? Still godly? Or taken to the Church as
more genteel?' Bulstrode's inner shrinkings and compromises are carica-
tured into blatant self-interest. And the torturer justifies his actions in
terms of the religion which has exploited him: 'you see, I was sent to
you, Nick — perhaps for a blessing to both of us?' But Raffles can only
act in the way he has been taught — by bribery and by parody. This is
why the conversations between the two men resolve themselves repeatedly into a statement followed by its mocking echo and why the whole
episode, which is Dickensian at a certain superficial level, brings us close
to the essential method of Dickens' later novels as two characters inti-
mately tied together by exploitation seek their independence through
further exploitation. Dialogue becomes echo as the exploiter addresses
his instrument. ' "So proud, so proud!" moaned Miss Havisham. ...
"Who taught me to be proud?" returned Estella ... "So hard, so hard!"
moaned Miss Havisham ... "Who taught me to be hard?" returned Estella.' In one sense, Bulstrode has made Raffles; it is *his* magic which has
conjured up this loud red figure, and now Raffles in revenge is about to
start remaking Bulstrode to suit himself. This is why the two men are so
closely tied to each other; they have each become the other's threaten-
ing extension. Between them they make up one person. This is how
Ladislaw their victim sees them when each man in turn seeks to make a
muddled kind of restitution. 'It seemed [to Ladislaw] like the fluctua-
tions of a dream — as if the action begun by that loud bloated stranger
were being carried on by this pale-eyed sickly-looking piece of respectability, whose subdued tone and glib formality of speech were at this

moment almost as repulsive to him as their remembered contrast'
(61:454). The two men thwart each other and remain as closely tied as
ever.

As Raffles now begins to assert himself he can only repeat the pattern of behaviour laid down by his exploiter. He must blackmail Bulstrode into becoming his passive agent and supplier of his fairly simple
needs — money, alcohol, and a certain amount of respectability. As Bulstrode falls into a more and more withered kind of paleness, Raffles
waxes more florid, more drunken, and more dictatorial. But he too is
preparing his own nemesis. Bulstrode knows he must regain some sem-
blance of freedom if he is to survive, and so, on Raffles' third visit he
reasserts himself by force of will and by invoking the world of law and
order which terrifies his old accomplice, already weakened by alcohol.
Now Raffles is as appalled as Bulstrode was on that evening at Stone
Court; the whole fabric of his life built upon extortion and blackmail is
threatened by this man who refuses to be intimidated. Gradually his religious scepticism is undermined — in the same way that Bulstrode's divine instrumentality is wavering in the balance. He feels himself being
hunted by the Devil who keeps transforming himself into Bulstrode,
young Nick his agent, and his last words describe the ground opening
under his feet as he is cast into hell. The two men are terrorising each
other into subjection — this leads them to reassert themselves — which
terrorises them even further. And in their desperate attempts to grapple
now with what they have previously denied they turn themselves into
the opposite of what they wish to be. When Raffles falls ill, however,
and Bulstrode tends him in his illness — the two men are inseparable
now — the banker makes a last effort to recover the sincerity of his
original hypothesis. Perhaps God's plan is to destroy his tormentor; he
sets 'himself to keep his intention separate from his desire' (70:516).
But it is too late, for Bulstrode knows that since they are feeding on
each other — one grows as the other withers — only one of them can
survive. The phrase used earlier in the novel — Bulstrode's 'vampire
feast of mastery' — now comes back with frightening force. As he sits
by the bed of his accomplice, Bulstrode 'had the air of an animated
corpse returned to movement without warmth' (70:516) and, as Raffles
sinks, Bulstrode comes back to life, drinking the blood of his agent, passive once more. And Raffles in his delirium senses his danger. Once

again Bulstrode tampers with the facts to nudge his hypothesis into reality; again he does it discreetly by suppressing rather than altering evidence, and in such a way that it is impossible to prove his guilt. But again he has been counterplotted by his tormentor who clings to him even after death. Raffles has already divulged his story (he too was seeking propitiation in his terror) and so the news of his death is clinching proof to the Middlemarch gossips of Bulstrode's guilt. They quickly put two and two together to make five, and the banker's subtle equivocations with his conscience come back to him as 'the full-grown fang of a discovered lie' (71:534). And he can't deny it. The man of God has been driven to commit murder to prove that he is a man of God – and then he has been abandoned.

Now all this, especially the glimpse of vampires feeding off each other, may seem a long way from the exact functioning of a scientific hypothesis. But I suggest that one leads to the other, that George Eliot's scientific conceits (those unliterary devices paraded in *Middlemarch*) lead logically to these monsters, vampires, and assorted succubi (the stock in trade of Gothic fiction) who live a subterranean metaphoric life beneath the provincial surface of the novel. The mind in its pride seeks to redeem by fiat the fallen world in which it lives, but instead turns it into an inferno where it is hunted down by monsters of its own creating. Although the relation between Raffles and Bulstrode is the most violent in the novel, I suggest that it can be seen as a paradigm, a clear means of understanding what is happening in several other important relations – those between Casaubon and Dorothea, and Lydgate and Rosamond, for example. The same pattern of tampering with the evidence of reality, of bribery and blackmail, the rapid escalation of demands on each side, plotting and counter-plotting, and finally open hostility. In each case, the monsters creep out of their holes at the end.

Casaubon marries Dorothea in order to transform the hostile world of men's thought into something not only docile and malleable, but also worshipping. He needs, like all academics, a captive audience and so he marries one. *She* want from Casaubon the binding theory his erudition seems to promise. Very quickly the passive agents turn active. Casaubon soon realizes that instead of getting 'a soft fence' against a hostile audience, he has married his most damaging critic who questions everything about him. She embodies and voices all those lingering

doubts and uncertainties he has sought to exclude, and finally he knows
that this unpaid amanuensis, instead of assisting him to finish his Key,
is fitting him critically into her own investigations and, in a parody of
his own research, seeing him and his actions 'too luminously as a part of
things in general' (42:306). For, of course, by this time Dorothea has
come to see his lifeless knowledge, which the binding theory was meant
to control, as an avalanche which is going to overwhelm her. Then begin
the plotting and counterplotting, Casaubon's heartattack caused by
Dorothea's resistance, and her desperation. Casaubon tries at first to
keep her from interfering in his work, but finally as death approaches
he decides to use her more directly. He will chain her irrevocably to his
pathetic brain-child. With her youthful assistance, which will continue
after his death, he can give his monumental labours 'a shape in which
they could be given to the world' (48:351). Again we have the idea of
someone seeking to draw life from another person; she is to work 'in a
virtual tomb, where there was the apparatus of a ghastly labour produc-
ing what would never see the light' (48:348). The images of ghostly and
illicit experiments multiply and parody the childbirth for which Dorothea longs. (By this time her compassion precludes any counterattack.)
Finally, just before Casaubon's death, she glimpses her future role in
terms as frightening as the vampires feeding. 'And now she pictured to
herself the days, the months, and years which she must spend in sorting
what might be called shattered mummies ... sorting them as food for a
theory which was already withered in the birth like an elfin child'
(48:351). Mr Casaubon has fathered upon his virgin sacrifice, from his
own barren brain (the metaphors become cluttered here), a deformed
dwarf of a hypothesis which she has to feed with the fragments of dead
bodies it needs to keep alive. All she wanted was a binding theory; all
he wanted was a docile wife.

Similarly, Lydgate dresses up that part of the material world which
his scientific acumen does not comprehend in the attractive shape of
Rosamond Vincy. *She* uses him to gain access to that world of rank,
that Eden where she will at last be fully appreciated. They each destroy
the other's plans and give birth to monsters. Lydgate by his exclusive
focus has created from the primitive tissue his own destroyer. He becomes Frankenstein (Middlemarch knows for certain that he has resus-
citated one dead body) hunted down by this inflexible monster who

submits him to his own experiments of maceration and control. For Rosamond too has quickly become disappointed; this handsome aristocrat with a will of his own is too interested in his science to lead her to heaven: his preoccupation with scientific subjects has become 'a morbid vampire's taste' (48:351). They force each other to commit acts against their own natures; just as Casaubon, the man of impeccable honour, was driven to leave a dishonourable will, so the man of science is driven to gambling and chance to keep at bay the material facts of life which Rosamond is now thrusting upon him. Rosamond, too, the epitome of what is becoming, is driven in desperation to her indiscretion with Ladislaw. By failing to disengage itself and its own interests from the world it is trying to understand, the mind turns an hypothesis into a deduction and spawns a brood of frightening creatures.

I wish finally to examine an episode in the novel where the mind instead of bringing about its own destruction, co-operates successfully with the external facts, creating meaning and redemption in the place of exploitation and fear. This episode in which Dorothea attempts to rescue Lydgate, Rosamond, Ladislaw, and herself, is the climax of *Middlemarch* and, although in many ways it is very emotional, its meaning is most clearly understood by the ideas of perception, hypothesis, and evidence. In this sequence of events we see Dorothea going ahead of the facts in an act of faith (another name for a hypothesis based upon probabilities) which brings meaning and understanding. She acts out the dialectic of Lydgate's research where the energy of the mind bathes the unintelligible evidence in its own ideally illuminated space. But now, of course, it is Dorothea who is examining the facts in order to help Lydgate who has been closely implicated in Bulstrode's disgrace. At first sight the evidence appears to be very damaging and Dorothea's friends advise caution. Farebrother knows that people can fall below their intention, and anyway in a situation like this it is very difficult to prove the opposite: 'there is no proof in favour of the man outside his own consciousness and assertion' (72:538). The facts are neutral and can be turned this way or that according to the viewer – and in Middlemarch they are usually turned to the worst possible meaning. Lydgate knows, as he says, that 'the circumstances would always be stronger than his

assertion' (73:541). And how can he assert his own innocence, even if
he were prepared to betray Bulstrode openly? The facts need a space
and a context in which they can be understood, and Dorothea with her
trust in Lydgate still unshaken can provide it. She sets off in her own
earnest and shortsighted way to see him.

And, at first, it all seems very simple. She expresses her trust in him
and his actions, and Lydgate for the first time enjoys the comfort of ex-
plaining and confessing all the circumstances to a sympathetic listener.
He is able to clarify to himself also the precise and subtle relation between the mind and the circumstances it was dealing with during Raffles' illness and death. Here the mind is recovering its integrity after a
lapse. But he can only do this in the illuminated space she provides. As
he says: 'I should like to tell you everything. It will be a comfort to me
to speak where belief has gone beforehand' (76:558). This act of belief,
it might be said, is different from the careful hypothesis which was
probing the meaning of the primitive tissue in his own laboratory. But
it is not very different. There too the facts could not speak for themselves, they too had to be vivified and given vital connection by the
mind, and the mind had to exclude its own interests in an act of disengagement. The additional dimension here is the way in which the external world (in the shape of another person) can respond to the hypothesis by which it is being interpreted and, if the hypothesis is close
enough to the facts, help to prove it true. This may sound an ungainly,
even a perverse way of talking about what is simply a question of sympathy and understanding between two people. My excuse is that George
Eliot encourages us to do this. Now, Lydgate begins to see that this al-
ternative hypothesis of his actions has validity, that he can be judged
in the wholeness of his character once more. As he accepts this he begins to regain his wholeness: he 'felt that he was recovering his old self
in the consciousness that he was with one who believed in it' (76:558).
Instead of being divided and dismembered, a character here is being put
together again. The valid hypothesis is transformed by Dorothea's nobility into the act of 'holding up an ideal for others in her believing conception of them' (77:565). This is the opposite of our earlier examples
where the self is threatened by those creatures it has created who
creep closer and closer, parodying and ridiculing. Here Dorothea

provides a secure area of freedom in which Lydgate can recover his old integrity.

The experiment has been so successful that Dorothea promises to visit Rosamond on the next day and explain everything to her. But in her eagerness she is becoming too optimistic, getting too far ahead of the facts, and when she stumbles upon Rosamond and Ladislaw in their compromising situation, her trust in human nature is shattered. The facts have destroyed the ideal image of Ladislaw, her most precious belief. There is the ideal conception of Ladislaw: here is the circumstantial evidence which has destroyed it. This is Dorothea's true test. Can she recover her earlier trusting state of mind now that Rosamond, the person she wished to help, has insinuated herself into her own most precious life? The passive recipient has again turned active with a vengeance.

After her night of grief, Dorothea begins to recover the calmness necessary for understanding. First she makes the initial act of disengaging the mind and its interests from what it is observing: she firmly puts aside the desire to see 'another's lot as an accident of [her] own' (80:577). The mind must move flexibly and disinterestedly among the circumstances, untrammelled by deduction. Then she begins to look at the evidence carefully. It is one of the most moving moments in the novel and it returns us to my opening point: the eyes and mind must scrutinize the facts diligently and carefully. But now the difficulties of doing so are overwhelming. George Eliot describes it in these terms: 'She began now to live through that yesterday morning deliberately again, forcing herself to dwell on every detail and its possible meaning. Was she alone in that scene? Was it her event only?' (80:577). The mind fighting to regain its composure must examine all the details and it must do so 'deliberately' — it is the adverb which is so impressive. Then she is forced to acknowledge that this *must* be a crisis in three other lives as well as her own, that her help is needed more than ever, and that her own grief is irrevelant except in so far as it is transformed into 'acquired knowledge' to help her to understand. Instead of excluding the circumstances which threaten her beliefs, she must absorb them into a more comprehensive hypothesis.

Dorothea's second visit to Rosamond has the conditions for a scene of mutual hostilities. Each thinks the other is the preferred woman, and certainly, says George Eliot, anyone knowing only 'the outer facts of the case' would wonder what Dorothea's purpose was in coming. But as she begins to talk Rosamond is reassured: she is not going to refer to the unbecoming situation of yesterday. Her tones 'seemed to flow with generous heedlessness above all the facts which had filled Rosamond's mind as grounds of obstruction' (81:581). Rosamond has her shattered pride to nurse, about which Dorothea knows nothing, just as Rosamond has no conception of the extent of Dorothea's love for Ladislaw. It is a situation ripe for mutual misunderstanding and destruction. Clearly the facts have to become known and explained if this is to be avoided but neither woman wants to mention them. And so, at first, Dorothea seeks to make Rosamond understand Lydgate's predicament and forgive and comfort him. But as she does so her own grief keeps rising and grappling her, obscuring the understanding and sympathy she needs to bring to this situation. She reasserts the facts to herself: 'this might be a turning-point in three lives – not in her own; no, there the irrevocable had happened' (81:582). Rosamond is impressed and softened as she listens. She is beginning to accept this new image of Lydgate which Dorothea is conjuring into reality, but there is resistance still. Dorothea knows she must speak about the entanglement with Ladislaw which must be removed if the marriage is to be saved. (Dorothea is in the dark here.) The unpleasant facts must be referred to, despite her own anguish, and she does so now, placing them meaningfully in the context of the experience of her own emotional life. It is the final hypothesis. First, from her life with Casaubon she talks of the difficulties of marriage – 'there is something even awful in the nearness that it brings' – and then when the moment cannot be avoided she refers obliquely to her own more recent shock of grief and the need sometimes to break away from strong ties: 'I know, I know that the feeling may be very dear – it has taken hold of us unawares – it is so hard, it may seem like death to part with it.' But at this moment her own grief which has been all along seeking to interfere rises and she feels 'as if she were being inwardly grappled. Here face had become a deathlier paleness' (81:584). As she struggles, we see the self trying to rise above itself and its own safety, even as it is threatened and dragged down. It is the act of the mind trying to disengage itself raised to the nth power – trying to jettison its own interests and yet transform all its experience into knowledge. It is a violent

moment of self-denial, disengagement, and death; in the novels it is frequently presented in images of crucifixion and this is certainly the
death Dorothea is dying as 'she struggles out of the waves of her own
sorrow.' The drama of Maggie Tulliver's similar action in the violence of
the flood has been absorbed by the metaphors. And the attempted act
of selfless disengagement redeems the unaccommodating facts which
Dorothea considered irrevocable. The experience has broken down even
Rosamond's resistance and in her 'pitying fellowship' at the sight of this
self-sacrifice, she tells Dorothea the true state of affairs. 'What you are
thinking is not true' (81:584). And they cling to each other, not in a
parasitic vampire's feast, but in mutual help. It is Rosamond's only act
of self-sacrifice but it is a crucial one for she is the only person able to
explain the truth of the situation. This discovery brings together again
and reconciles the two clashing images in Dorothea's mind, her ideal
concept of Ladislaw and the circumstances in which she discovered
him. They are no longer contradictory; and Dorothea in her grief has
discovered her true passion for Ladislaw, who can now be brought out
from among the tall white lilies into the light of common day, where
other women might try to compromise him, where she will marry him,
and then learn the price of butter. But in that one moment with Rosamond the irrevocable facts were redeemed from their fallen, fragmented, misunderstood state. The inspired hypothesis, modified in the
process, has brought them into conformity with itself and the outer
world has become an extension of Dorothea's wishes.

These, then, are the two very distinct worlds of the novel: one in
which monsters pursue their devilish creators and dwarfs feed upon dismembered human bodies, the other in which the fragmented world of
external fact is vivified, redeemed, and Eden is recovered. My point is
that the only thing which separates one from the other in the first place
is the unexciting, undramatic moment when the mind disengages itself
from its own interests and tests its hypothesis impartially against the
facts. From this basis the mind can then move into a genuine relation
with the outer world, whether in the form of scientific investigation or
of a sympathetic relation with another person. But, if the act of disengagement is not made, then even in respectable, provincial Middlemarch
the vampires are waiting to perch on one's shoulder.

GILLIAN BEER

Myth and the single consciousness: *Middlemarch* and *The Lifted Veil*

Writing on 5 December 1859 just after her first reading of Darwin's *Origin of Species* George Eliot exclaimed: 'So the world gets on step by step towards brave clearness and honesty! But to me the Development theory and all other explanations of processes by which things came to be, produce a feeble impression compared with the mystery that lies under the processes.'[1] George Eliot never abandoned a sense of something always there, quiet, beneath consciousness, a part of that resignation which oscillates with activity to compose our life. Evolution; progress; historicism; positivism with its emphasis on cause and effect: since the mid-nineteenth century these ideas have provided dominant patterns for understanding experience. They all substitute sequence for the eternal present of religious faith and of romance. Evolutionary theory in particular has achieved a power over men's imagination like that of a myth in a period of belief. George Eliot's novels delight in the multiplicity inherent in all such systems, but she continued to feel a longing, if not for the transcendent, at least for the numinous, the incandescent, the mysterious. This mystery may express itself either as celebration or as latency: latency in its double aspect of concealment and futurity. In *Middlemarch* the Nazarene Naumann's paintings 'expanded that grand conception of supreme events as mysteries at which the successive ages were spectators, and in relation to which the great souls of all periods become as it were contemporaries' (22:158). In

The Lifted Veil, finished nine months before her remarks on Darwin were written, Latimer, the narrator-hero, sees the need for mystery as the creative force in human behaviour:

So absolute is our soul's need of something hidden and uncertain for the maintenance of that doubt and hope and effort which are the breath of its life, that if the whole future were laid bare to us beyond today, the interest of mankind would be bent on the hours that lie between; we should pant after the uncertainties of our one morning and our one afternoon ... Conceive the condition of the human mind if all propositions whatsoever were self-evident except one, which was to become self-evident at the close of a summer's day, but in the meantime might be the subject of question, of hypothesis, of debate. Art and philosophy, literature and science, would fasten like bees on that one proposition which had the honey of probability in it, and be the more eager because their enjoyment would end with sunset. (2:318)

In this macabre and depressive story she burdens her hero with a double weight of insight: he can see into other consciousnesses and he can see the future. The claustrophobic atmosphere of *The Lifted Veil* is intensified by making Latimer's frail and diseased sensibility both the experiencer and the interpreter: he is imprisoned within a world in which no creative action is possible because everything is foreseen and nothing can be altered. He falls in love with Bertha, the 'water-nixie' woman he marries, because her consciousness alone is veiled to him: 'no matter how empty the adytum, so that the veil be thick enough' (2:318). The veil is lifted as her empty consciousness becomes filled with hatred of him.

Throughout her career George Eliot was fascinated by differing types of vision and insight, and particularly by those of the scientist and the writer. Latimer is anti-scientific. In his childhood he has been force-fed with science in one of those educational schemes so beloved and hated in the eighteen-forties and fifties (the 'systems' to which John Stuart Mill and Meredith's Richard Feverel were submitted are obvious examples): 'I was hungry for human deeds and human emotions, so I was to be plentifully crammed with the mechanical powers, the elementary bodies, and the phenomena of electricity and magnetism'

(1:283). He does not wish to know reasons *why*. His is essentially a lyri-
cal consciousness: Jean Jacques Rousseau is his mentor. He cannot
make relationships: he turns to nature for succour. 'My least solitary
moments were those in which I pushed off in my boat, at evening, towards the centre of the lake; it seemed to me that the sky, and the
glowing mountain-tops, and the wide blue water, surrounded me with a
cherishing love such as no human face had shed on me since my mother's love had vanished out of my life' (1:284). His alienated, self-pitying
imagination images all the inhibitions of Romanticism without its creativity. But also included in the story is his one friend and opposite, the
natural scientist and physician Charles Meunier who disappears from
the story before Latimer's gift of divination is made manifest. He reappears at the end and performs the scientific experiment which provides
the story's lurid climax. He gives a blood-transfusion to Bertha's maid
which revives her from death long enough to denounce her mistress's
plan to poison Latimer. (The episode reminds one of the strong influence of Hawthorne in George Eliot's early career. The whole story has a
kinship in atmosphere with works like 'Dr Heidegger's Experiment.')
Charles Meunier is seen as sober, stable, actively experimental, as
against the manic-depressive, passively receptive disposition of Latimer.
In some ways he foreshadows Lydgate, and the story of Lydgate and
Laure in *Middlemarch* has a garish extremity much more like *The
Lifted Veil* than like the rest of *Middlemarch.* Similarly, Bertha and
Rosamond look alike with their tranquil blonde beauty and both share
the same calculating constriction of personality which seems decorous
compliancy to the men they marry. But in *Middlemarch* personality is
not held in perpetual *rigor mortis* as here. The future includes potential
(Rosamond can briefly break out of the set pattern of her personality);
in *The Lifted Veil* all future and all interiority is hideously transfixed
and truncated. It is divined with absolute authority by a single limited
consciousness.

In the fashionable para-sciences of the mid-Victorian period (mes-
merism and phrenology) there is a strong element of divination. Latimer as a child is affronted by the phrenologist who reads his head ('as if
he would cheapen it.' Divination is also a function of the doctor and of
the novelist. The novelist must divine other consciousnesses and project
the future. At the same time, novels — and particularly novels set back

in the past — imprison the future. The solitary creator remains aware of the solipsism of the world he makes, though it may look open and fruitful to the reader. In her work George Eliot constantly seeks *relations*, ways beyond the single consciousness. And this implies ways beyond not only the single consciousness of any character in the novel, but beyond that of the novelist himself. By studying *The Lifted Veil* alongside *Middlemarch* we can come to a fuller knowledge of the ways George Eliot sought out beyond the 'desolate loneliness' of single consciousness. In *The Mill on the Floss* she emphasizes the moral congruity of the artist and the scientist in their search for understanding: 'In natural science, I have understood, there is nothing petty to the mind that has a large vision of relations, as to which every single object suggests a vast sum of conditions. It is surely the same with the observations of human life' (VI 1:6). In *Middlemarch* she contrasts Lydgate's scientific inspiration with the sensational representationalism which is a typical failing in later 'naturalistic' fiction:

Many men have been praised as vividly imaginative on the strength of their profuseness in indifferent drawing or cheap narration: — reports of very poor talk going on in distant orbs; or portraits of Lucifer coming down on his bad errands as a large ugly man with bat's wings and spurts of phosphorescence; or exaggerations of wantonness that seem to reflect life in a diseased dream. But these kinds of inspiration Lydgate regarded as rather vulgar and vinous compared with the imagination that reveals subtle actions inaccessible by any sort of lens, but tracked in that outer darkness through long pathways of necessary sequence by the inward light which is the last refinement of Energy, capable of bathing even the ethereal atoms in its ideally illuminated space. (16:122)

As Mr Brooke timidly and succinctly puts it: 'I went into science a great deal myself at one time; but I saw it would not do. It leads to everything ...' (One should always pay attention to Mr Brooke.)

In *The Lifted Veil* George Eliot projects with a nightmare indirection many of the anxieties which assail her particular creativity. The story images her intermittent doubts about her role as a maker of fictions. Two months after the publication of the last volume of *Middlemarch* in December 1872, Blackwood wrote to ask if he could republish

The Lifted Veil 'in a proposed New Series of Tales from Blackwood.'[2]
He had been distressed by it when it first appeared in *Blackwood's Magazine* in July 1859 and wrote to her in May of that year: 'I think you must have been worrying and disturbing yourself about something when you wrote it.'[3] In asking now to republish it he speaks of it as 'this striking although horribly painful story.' George Eliot replies:

Apropos of the Lifted Veil, I think it will not be judicious to reprint it at present. I care for the idea which it embodies and which justifies its painfulness. A motto which I wrote on it yesterday perhaps is a sufficient indication of that idea.

'Give me no light, great heaven, but such as turns
To energy of human fellowship;
No powers save the growing heritage
That makes completer manhood.'

But it will be well to put the story in harness with some other productions of mine, and not send it forth in its dismal loneliness. There are many things in it which I would willingly say over again, and I shall never put them in any other form. But we must wait a little.[4]

In the motto which she provides for the story with the experience of writing *Middlemarch* behind her, George Eliot attempts to stabilize its meaning in acceptably positive terms. She adopts the imagery of the scientific imagination: light turns to human energy; the evolutionary process amasses new potentialities for man. She has moved a long way from her original self-defensive introduction of it to Blackwood: 'I have a slight story of an outre kind − not a *jeu d'esprit*, but a *jeu de melancolie* ... I think nothing of it, but my private critic says it is very striking and original, and on the strength of that opinion, I mention it.'[5] In 1872, despite her graver sense of the story's significance ('There are many things in it which I would willingly say over again, and I shall never put them in any other form'), she is still uneasy about it. The fact that she still felt sufficiently threatened by the work to refuse republication thirteen years after it was written suggests that it gives expression to emotional and artistic problems barely under her control. Many of these problems find some kind of an answer in the 'positive' world of *Middlemarch* in which the simultaneity of human lots creates its own form of prophecy, and the only future life is our future here.[6]

In such a world science and mythology perform humanist functions: they bind perceptions together and they enrich with meaning the recurrences of human experience; they allow at once for exploration and mystery; they include the recognition of latent or immanent worlds 'tracked in that outer darkness through long pathways of necessary sequence by the inward light which is the last refinement of Energy.' 'Effective magic' writes the narrator 'is transcendent nature.' Although George Eliot early rejected the supernatural, she remained in two minds about the preternatural. In the same letter that she sent *The Lifted Veil* to Blackwood she suggests an alteration to the willow wand episode in *Adam Bede* for the third edition to show that it might be possible to reduce it to natural elements but 'in our eagerness to explain impressions, we often lose our hold of the sympathy that comprehends them.' Again, there is the reluctance to abandon mystery as an element in human experience.[7]

At the end of her career, in *Daniel Deronda*, she returns to the theme of second sight: 'it is a matter of knowledge that there are persons whose yearnings, conceptions — nay, travelled conclusions — continually take the form of images which have a foreshadowing power: the deed they would do starts up before them in complete shape, making a coercive type; the event they hunger for or dread rises into vision with a seed-like growth, feeding itself fast on unnumbered impressions' (38:295). But by then second sight can function as creative prophecy: 'the fuller nature desires to be an agent, to create, and not merely to look on' (38:301). In *The Lifted Veil* insight is intransitive. There is no replenishing reciprocity between Latimer and the world. He sees into others and into the future with scarified bareness. He is endowed with a poet's sensibility without a poet's assured creativity. 'A poet pours forth his song and *believes* in the listening ear and answering soul, to which his song will be floated sooner or later' (1:284). Latimer sees passively, without any hope of reciprocity or of loving audience: 'weary of incessant insight and foresight, without delusions and without hope' (1:277). His will is paralysed by his prescience.

Latimer's situation hideously figures forth and parallels the trials of the novelist: his powers express the determinism and solipsism latent in

the act of writing fiction. The single self of the writer can see within
and beyond the characters. He contains their future; they exist only
within his own creativity unless a relation can be engendered between
writer and reader.

The reader is the living variable within the fictive world. That warm
and urgent tone of the narrator addressing us in George Eliot's novels is
a kind of wooing of the 'real' world beyond; our involvement is necessary not only to educate *us* but to sustain the writer ontologically. At
the beginning of her career George Eliot was the 'hidden self' of Marian
Evans.[8] In *Adam Bede* she dramatized the masculinity of the narrator:
'God preserve you and me from being the beginners of such misery!' he
writes, of Hetty's pregnancy. In *The Lifted Veil* the narrator and the
hero is a frail, depressive man (something of the same figure recurs in
more fortunate circumstances in the old bachelor narrator of *The Impressions of Theophrastus Such*). In *Middlemarch* the open, brooding,
androgynous presence of the narrator allows for a full range of intellectual and emotional response beyond the confines of the characters.
George Eliot went through periods of loss of faith in her powers as an
artist, particularly after just finishing a book.[9] The picture of a stifled,
yearning sensibility with no outlet, no achievement, no communication,
only a horribly arid power of divination and prescience reveals a world
in which insight has stripped away mystery and discovered only the
humdrum. It is as if the writer is exploring the desolating realization
that the apparently ordinary may be merely ordinary, that all creative
sympathy and energy may finally be baulked by the trivial. It's a problem she had tackled in the characterization of Hetty in *Adam Bede* and
she had there found a way through by making Hetty's tragedy a physical one. In *Scenes of Clerical Life* she had already explored the dowdi-
ness of life, and alleviated it by flashes of melodrama. Despite the lurid
atmosphere of *The Lifted Veil* the horror at the centre of the story is
the horror of littleness, of the estranged self pressed upon and violated
by 'the trivial experience of indifferent people' – and worse, 'by the
souls of those who were in a close relation to me.'

when the rational talk, the graceful attentions, the wittily-turned
phrases, and the kindly deeds, which used to make the web of their
characters, were seen as if thrust asunder by a microscopic vision, that

showed all the intermediate frivolities, all the suppressed egoism, all the struggling chaos of puerilities, meanness, vague capricious memories, and indolent make-shift thoughts, from which human words and deeds emerge like leaflets covering a fermenting heap. (1:295)

Latimer sees into his brother's underconsciousness and discovers with hatred only conceit and patronage revealed 'in all their naked skinless complication.' The image simultaneously suggests embryo and abortion. In *Middlemarch* it is Mr Casaubon whose personality comes closest to that of Latimer:

To know intense joy without a strong bodily frame, one must have an enthusiastic soul. Mr Casaubon had never had a strong bodily frame, and his soul was sensitive without being enthusiastic: it was too languid to thrill out of self-consciousness into passionate delight ... it was that proud narrow sensitiveness which has not mass enough to spare for transformation into sympathy, and quivers thread-like in small currents of self-preoccupation or at best of an egoistic scrupulosity. (29:206)

The need to discover and to make believable the quiddity, the in-eluctable mystery within people beyond their apparent ordinariness, was what gave moral meaning to George Eliot's career as a novelist concerned with 'realism' rather than 'idealism.'[10] In *Middlemarch* the structural parallels are in reality less parallels than a web suggesting a multiple reality released from the single self of the writer. In *The Lifted Veil* we have only the single, authoritative self-pitying insight of Latimer to guide our reading of the world. Latimer is oppressed and wearied by the pressure of other equally self-regarding consciousnesses with which he can feel no living connection.

Dorothea's ghostly return to Lowick Manor is described in a depressive language similar to that of Latimer: 'All existence seemed to beat with a lower pulse than her own, and her religious faith was a solitary cry, the struggle out of a nightmare in which every object was withering and shrinking away from her. Each remembered thing in the room was disenchanted, was deadened as an unlit transparency ...' (28:202). But shortly afterwards the author pulls herself sharply away from Dorothea: 'One morning, some weeks after her arrival at Lowick, Dorothea

— but why always Dorothea?' George Eliot shares with Fielding a
distrust of the autobiographical focus, with its assumption that the
single point of view is truer than that of the historian. Fielding points
out in *Joseph Andrews* that autobiography (whether fictional or actual,
Pamela or Colley Cibber) is always polemical and partial. George Eliot,
while modestly pretending not to follow his example of 'copious remarks and digressions' speaks of herself as a 'belated historian' after
his example. Using again that imagery of the web with its inherent
'relations' rather than singleness, she writes:

I at least have so much to do in unravelling certain human lots, and
seeing how they were woven and interwoven, that all the light I can
command must be concentrated on this particular web, and not
dispersed over that tempting range of relevancies called the universe.
(15:105)

Three quotations bring out the problem of the hypersensitive consciousness, common to the creative writer and to the preternaturally
gifted. Latimer:

— my diseased participation in other people's consciousness continued
to torment me; now it was my father, and now my brother, now Mrs
Filmore or her husband, and now our German courier, whose stream of
thought rushed upon me like a ringing in the ears not to be got rid of,
though it allowed my own impulses and ideas to continue their uninter-
rupted course. It was like a preternaturally heightened sense of hearing,
making audible to one a roar of sound where others find perfect
stillness. (1:301)

In *Middlemarch:*

That element of tragedy which lies in the very fact of frequency, has
not yet wrought itself into the coarse emotion of mankind; and perhaps
our frames could hardly bear much of it. If we had a keen vision and
feeling of all ordinary human life, it would be like hearing the grass
grow and the squirrel's heart beat, and we should die of the roar which
lies on the other side of silence. (20:144)

Caleb Garth is sufficiently stable to find a music in the heterogenous roar of society at work:

the indispensable might of that myriad-headed, myriad-handed labour by which the social body is fed, clothed and housed. It had laid hold of his imagination in boyhood. The echoes of the great hammer where roof or keel were a-making, the signal-shouts of the workmen, the roar of the furnace, the thunder and plash of the engine, were a sublime music to him ... (24:185)

Ian Adam has called attention to a passage in T.H. Huxley's essay 'The Physical Basis of Life,' published in *The Fortnightly Review*, February 1869,[11] which illustrates the dullness of human senses in this way:

the wonderful noonday silence of a tropical forest is, after all, due only to the dulness of our hearing; and could our ears catch the murmur of those tiny Maelstroms, as they whirl in the innumerable myriads of living cells which constitute each tree, we should be stunned, as with the roar of a great city.

In each case the imagery is drawn from intense sound. George Eliot, as the passage from *The Lifted Veil* makes clear, had already recognized very early in her career the particular disease of the Victorian consciousness: hyperaesthesia.

The ethic of realism — paying respect to things as they are, accepting the objectivity of objects — combined with the ethic of sympathy descending from the Romantics, resulted in near intolerable pressure on the receptive or penetrating consciousness from the external world, the world of others. Ruskin's creativity is the central example. When Ruskin instructs us to lie down on the next bank the detailism is made pleasurable by 'mystery' again:

... the cluster of leaves and grass close to your face ... a mystery of soft shadow in the depths of the grass, with indefinite forms of leaves, which you cannot trace nor count, within it, and out of that, the nearer leaves coming in every subtle gradation of tender light and flickering form, quite beyond the delicacy of pencilling to follow; and yet you will rise up from that bank ... and profess to represent it by a few blots of 'forcible' foreground colour.[12]

Dickens deals with this problem by mythologizing it and presenting an animistic world; Meredith transposes the thronging pressures into metaphor and so holds them at a distance. But a painfully direct sense of other selves and of the organic nature of society is at the basis of George Eliot's creativity. Latimer provides a nightmare image of the burden of seeing into other consciousnesses and foreseeing the future as the novelist must do. She has to find a way to prevent herself from being deafened by the insurgency of objects and of others. Yet she must believe in the value of others if she is not to be diminished. Hyperaesthesia leaves the perceiver without a barrier between himself and the perceived. This is one aspect of Latimer's dilemma. Hyperaesthesia is not a mutual condition − it implies no response from the outer world. That is another element in his desolation. Latimer's dilemma, in its mixture of determinism, solipsism, and hyperaesthesia corresponds to the perils latent in George Eliot's situation as a novelist.

In *Middlemarch* she seeks out ways beyond the single consciousness. She creates a sense of inclusiveness and extension. Nothing is end-stopped. Multiplicity is developed through the open relation created between narrator and reader, through participation in the immanent worlds of others and through the unlimited worlds of ideas. When she uses the image of the microscope in *Middlemarch* there is no suggestion of condescension to ways of being more minute in scale: rather there is a recognition of the multiple unseen worlds by which we are surrounded and which new methods of perception may reveal without reducing the mystery inherent in the fact of multiplicity. Simultaneity of experiences is the equivalent in the novelist's art, and *Middlemarch* is enriched by a sense of multiple latent relations which are permitted to remain latent.

Significant repetition and variation is an essential principle in the structure of *Middlemarch*. Science and mythology create within the work ways beyond the single into a shared, anonymous, and therefore more deeply creative knowledge.[13] Myth, in particular, offers the continuity of collective insight against the anomie of the solitary perceiver. It is with the uses of myth as a means of enriching the

concept of 'relations' that I shall be chiefly concerned in the
argument that follows.

Middlemarch the book is something different from Middlemarch the
town. It's worth emphasizing this simple primary distinction because
the inhabitants of Middlemarch within the book are so confident that
Middlemarch is not only in the Midlands but in the Middle of the
world; the book's expansiveness creates an effect of size for the town,
so that Paris, Rome, and London look thin and small by comparison.
But we as readers are made also to recognize its mediocrity. George
Eliot herself, after all, escaped from Middlemarch and her business as
narrator in the novel is to remind us of worlds intellectual, aesthetic,
spiritual, which do not naturally flourish in the provinces. Not only the
individual selves but the collective social self of Middlemarch is framed
and placed. She creates a double time within the novel – the 'now' of
herself and her first readers and the 'now-then' of the late eighteen
twenties. The intellectual concerns of the people and period within the
novel are carefully dated and set in relation to her own time. This relation is often ironic, as in her treatment of the Reform Bill, sometimes
prophetic, as in the imagery drawn from the development of the microscope, and occasionally a fusing of the values of several times, as in the
opening sentence of chapter 1 which makes of Dorothea a genuinely
pre-Raphaelite Madonna.[14]

The typical concern of the intellectual characters in the book is with
visions of unity, but a unity which seeks to resolve the extraordinary
diversities of the world back into a single answer: the key to all mythologies, the primitive tissue, allegorical painting (Ladislaw mocks Naumann: 'I do *not* think that all the universe is straining towards the ob-
scure significance of your pictures' [19:141]). Casaubon and Dorothea,
for different reasons, are distressed by the miscellaneity of Rome,
where the remains of different cultures are all topographically jostling
each other, apparently without hierarchy of meaning:

She had been led through the best galleries, and had been taken to the
chief points of view, had been shown the greatest ruins and the most
glorious churches, and she had ended by oftenest choosing to drive out
to the Campagna where she could feel alone with the earth and sky,
away from the oppressive masquerade of ages, in which her own

life too seemed to become a masque with enigmatical costumes.
(20:143)

Much later in the book, at the great crisis of her life, that earth and sky
are peopled in the dawn with impersonal permanent figures, characteristic of human destiny in their ordinariness and their mystery: 'On the
road there was a man with a bundle on his back and a woman carrying
her baby; in the field she could see figures moving – perhaps the shepherd with his dog' (80:578). In that image of the family (though we are
not certain that it is a family) and of the possible shepherd there are
echoes of Christian mythology – but it is here diffused and brought
down to earth. These are valuable figures because, simply, they are
human figures each pursuing his own concerns: 'she felt the largeness
of the world and the manifold wakings of men to labour and endur-
ance.' The numinous must express itself in this book through the
human solely. Myths – the groping religious and proto-scientific perceptions of differing cultures – survive because they tell stories about
human or quasi-human figures which satisfy the need for recurrence.
Cultures are defined by their myths but myths outlive the culture
which produced them. Casaubon's dry collation of myth, arranged according to the authenticity of their 'period,' is set against George Eliot's
own rich, manifold, free-ranging invocation of diverse mythologies
within the book.

Latimer felt the distress of the poet manqué: 'the poet's sensibility
without his voice ... this dumb passion brings with it a fatal solitude of
soul in the society of one's fellow-men.' (1:284) In *Middlemarch* Ladislaw offers a definition of the poet which emphasizes outgoing creativity
as opposed to receptive hypersensitivity:

'To be a poet is to have a soul so quick to discern, that no shade of
quality escapes it, and so quick to feel, that discernment is but a hand
playing with finely-ordered variety on the chords of emotion – a soul
in which knowledge passes instantaneously into feeling, and feeling
flashes back as a new organ of knowledge. One may have that condition
by fits only.

Dorothea retorts:

'But you leave out the poems. I think they are wanted to complete the poet. I understand what you mean about knowledge passing into feeling, for that seems to be just what I experience. But I am sure I could never produce a poem.'

'You *are* a poem — and that is to be the best part of a poet — what makes up the poet's consciousness in his best moods,' said Will, showing such originality as we all share with the morning and the spring-time and other endless renewals. (22:166)

The tone of the narrator's comment is tenderly playful but what is being said is crucial to our understanding. Dorothea is an embodiment of poetry. Will's response has the originality of 'endless renewals.' What he says sheds light also on the relationship between Casaubon and Dorothea. Casaubon cannot accept the protean nature of myth because renewal and embodiment are beyond his imaginative grasp. Dorothea may be a poem to Ladislaw; she is never, in any sense, myth to Casaubon.

Casaubon is in a sense judged by myth. (The original bearer of his name, the seventeenth-century Casaubon, had written a treatise *against* John Dee, the Elizabethan necromantic scientist who believed he had discovered the key to the universe.) The acquisitive sensibility tabulates, collects, and reduces; the creative sensibility has the responsibility not only of perceiving but of *making* connections. In Dorothea knowledge and feeling actively generate each other. So she can learn; he must withdraw from learning. We see this particularly clearly in their attitude to art and Christian legend, as I hope to show later.

Instead of the desolate privacy of the Romantic ego, or the moral types of neo-classicism, George Eliot is seeking communal insights. At this stage I call warningly to mind the narrator's remark: 'Probabilities are as various as the faces to be seen at will in fretwork or paper-hangings: every form is there, from Jupiter to Judy, if you only look with creative inclination' (32:224). But even here the indications are nicely poised: the vagrant action of the imagination discovers Jupiter and Judy simultaneously — experience has many faces; probabilities are a type of freedom; Jupiter and Judy are both products of the communal imagination. In *Middlemarch* the narrator weaves into commentary, dialogue, and metaphor, allusions to a great number of mythological systems: classical myth, folk tale and theatre, Troubadour romance and courtly love, the Arabian Nights, hagiography, mythography, the Brothers Grimm's collections, Christian legend and martyrology. Most of them are unemphatically placed, not seeming to demand a contextual alertness from the reader. But if we explore the context the allusions always yield fruitful insights which replenish our understanding of the accord between any individual's experience and the lived world of others. They express mysteries in relation to which 'the great souls of all periods become as it were contemporaries.'

So, for example, a little earlier in the scene between Ladislaw and Dorothea where he tells her that she is a poem, he has accused her of wanting to be a martyr:

I suspect that you have some false belief in the virtues of misery, and want to make your life a martyrdom ... You talk as if you had never known any youth. It is monstrous — as if you had a vision of Hades in your youth, like the boy in the legend. You have been brought up in some of those horrible notions that choose the sweetest women to devour — like Minotaurs. (22:163)

Ladislaw's verbal energy readily shifts dead metaphor into myth: (monstrous becomes Minotaur). Before pursuing the Minotaur, however, that other, less familiar, allusion is worth pondering. Who was the boy in the legend? and how does he relate to the idea of martyrdom? The answer seems to be that he was Anskar, a ninth-century missionary to Scandinavia, whose life was recorded in a biography by Bishop Rimbert, his fellow missionary and successor.[15] In Ladislaw's summary the story of him losing his youth through seeing a vision of Hades sounds like a German romantic legend; in the biography (chapter 2) it appears as the first of a series of visions which come to Anskar. At five years' old 'having given himself up to boyish levity' he sees his dead mother in a troup of ladies surrounding the Virgin Mary: he is fixed 'in a miry and slippery place, from which he could not escape with great difficulty.' He is told by the Virgin that if he wishes to escape and come to his mother he must 'flee every kind of vanity, and put away childish jests and have regard to the seriousness of life ... Immediately after this vision he began to be serious and to avoid childish associations, and to devote himself

more constantly to reading and meditation and other useful occupa-
tions ...' But there is more to it than this pathetic story, which on its
own would not clinch the connection. The most important of Anskar's
visions, when he had just become a monk in his teens, promised him the
crown of martyrdom.[16] The rest of his long and active life, much involved in reform of his order and in missionary activities, was spent in
the expectation of martyrdom. When, in old age, he realized that he
was dying of dysentery, he was inconsolable, though his disciple
pointed out that his whole life of service and self-chastisement had been
a martyrdom. He was granted a revelation which seen without the eye
of faith might seem unremarkable but which gave him assurance. A
voice said, 'Believe firmly and in no wise doubt that God of his grace
will grant both favours, that is, He will forgive the sins concerning
which you are anxious, and will accomplish all that He promised' (chapter 40). So he died in his bed, finally full of faith in God's purpose: his
martyrdom was not to be a martyr. This curiously Jamesian tale lies
buried beneath that allusion of Ladislaw's. Its beautiful appropriateness
to Dorothea's problems and fate is complete but latent. It is an extraordinary example of the profuse organic creativity of *Middlemarch* that
George Eliot could afford *not* to bring it to the surface: that she could
allow the mystery of relations to persist.

　In the Prelude George Eliot offers the image of the infant Saint
Theresa 'walking forth one morning hand-in-hand with her still smaller
brother, to go and seek martyrdom in the country of the Moors.' She
rejects 'the many-volumed romances of chivalry.' She does not achieve
martyrdom: 'She found her epos in the reform of a religious order.'
Dorothea is to achieve neither martyrdom nor reform — except indirectly through Ladislaw's reforming journalism. So we move from the
hagiographic to the transformational fairy-tale image of the ugly duckling: 'Here and there a cygnet is reared uneasily among the ducklings in
the brown pond, and never finds the living stream in fellowship with its
own oary-footed kind.' Hans Andersen's tale is given a further melancholy modulation here: the swan must continue to live surrounded by
ducks on the brown pond. Hans Andersen's refined, psychological,
faintly sadistic art is a part of the post-Romantic world which George
Eliot and her readers inhabited. His work was first translated in the
eighteen forties; it post-dates the world described in the novel when

'Romanticism, which has helped to fill some dull blanks with love and knowledge, had not yet penetrated the times with its leaven and entered into everybody's food; it was fermenting still as a distinguishable vigorous enthusiasm in certain long-haired German artists at Rome' (19:140).

George Eliot uses this double-time structure on more than one occasion: and in particular in the Ariadne/Cleopatra figure. She also uses diverse mythological structures simultaneously; in particular the lives of the saints and classical myth. She was indebted particularly to Mrs Jameson for her full realization of the value of 'Christian legends or fairy tales.' George Eliot knew Mrs Jameson personally. She used her *Legends of the Monastic Orders* (1850) and *Legends of the Madonna* (1852) while she was writing *Romola*. And Mrs Jameson's *Sacred and Legendary Art* (1848) has particular significance for *Middlemarch*. Mrs Jameson's main contention in that book is that in the mythology of the saints we have a visual and symbolic language equivalent in intensity to classical myth.

I hate the destructive as I revere the progressive spirit. We must laugh if anyone were to try and persuade us that the sun was guided along his blazing path by 'a fair-haired god who touched a golden lyre,' but shall we therefore cease to adore in the Apollo Belvedere the majestic symbol of light, the most divine impersonation of intellectual power and beauty? So of the corresponding Christian symbols: − may that time never come, when we shall look up at the effigy of the winged and radiant angel trampling down the brute-fiend without a glow of faith in the perpetual supremacy and final triumph of good over evil.

She contrasts the knowledge of classical myth with the general ignorance of the symbolism of medieval Christian legend in a way likely to discomfit the modern reader:

Who ever confounds Venus with a Minerva, or a Vestal with an Amazon; or would endure an undraped Juno, or a beardless Jupiter? ... but ... We learn to know St Francis by his brown habit and shaven crown and wasted ardent features: but how do we distinguish him from St Anthony, or St Dominick?[17]

George Eliot takes up Mrs Jameson's point quite directly at the beginning of chapter nineteen where she is discussing the coming of Romanticism and the deliberately religious, symbolic art of the Nazarenes whom many art-historians see as the precursors of the Pre-Raphaelite movement.

Travellers did not often carry full information on Christian art either in their heads or their pockets; and even the most brilliant English critic of the day [Hazlitt] mistook the flower-flushed tomb of the ascended Virgin for an ornamental vase due to the painter's fancy. (19:139)

She expects her readers of the eighteen-seventies to register the start of a movement which opened a system of symbolism vital to the sensibility of their own time. What seems decorative to the ignorant eye is part of a far-ranging, implicit system of meaning: that had been Mrs Jameson's central point too.

In the very next paragraph George Eliot presents 'a young man whose hair ... was abundant and curly ... who had just turned his back on the Belvedere Torso in the Vatican.' The Apollonian figure is, of course, Will Ladislaw. Then, beside 'the reclining Ariadne, then called the Cleopatra,' the two men see 'a breathing, blooming girl whose form, not shamed by the Ariadne, was clad in Quakerish grey drapery ...' (19:140). In the description of Dorothea the double-time system enters again: the knowledge that the figure is Ariadne is historically beyond the reach of the characters but is invoked by George Eliot as part of the shared world-knowledge of herself and her reader: Ladislaw, the bringer of cultural tidings, as so often, is given a midway status; it is he who two chapters later brings into the open the idea of Dorothea 'brought up in some of the horrible notions that choose the sweetest women to devour — like Minotaurs.' To Naumann she is 'antique form animated by Christian sentiment — a sort of Christian Antigone — sensuous force controlled by spiritual passion' (19:141). But if she is related in terms of classical myth to Ariadne she is also Dorothea.[18] She cannot become a St Theresa. Who then was St Dorothea? The answer is to be found in the second volume of Mrs Jameson's work.[19] St Dorothea was both a martyr and a spiritual bride.

She was then led forth to death; and, as she went, a young man, a law-yer of the city named Theophilus, who had been present when she was first brought before the governor, called to her mockingly: 'Ha! fair maiden, goest thou to join thy bridegroom? Send me, I pray thee, of the fruits and flowers of that same garden of which thou hast spoken: I would fain taste of them!' And Dorothea looking on him inclined her head with a gentle smile, and said: 'Thy request, O Theophilus, is granted!' Whereat he laughed aloud with his companions; but she went on cheerfully to death.

When she came to the place of execution, she knelt down and prayed: and suddenly appeared at her side a beautiful boy, with hair bright as sunbeams:

A smooth-faced glorious thing,

With thousand blessings dancing in his eyes.

In his hand he held a basket containing three apples, and three fresh-gathered and fragrant roses. She said to him: 'Carry these to Theo-philus; say that Dorothea hath sent them, and that I go before him to the garden when they came, and await him there.' With these words she bent her neck and received the death-stroke.

Meantime the angel (for it was an angel) went to seek Theophilus, and found him still laughing in merry mood over the idea of the pro-mised gift. The angel placed before him the basket of celestial fruit and flowers, saying: 'Dorothea sends thee this,' and vanished. What words can express the wonder of Theophilus?

The 'beautiful boy, with hair bright as sunbeams,' bringer of fruit and flowers, seems a familiar figure. Within the novel Ladislaw appropriates most of the images of sunlight, issuing perhaps not only from Apollo but from St Dorothea's 'smooth-faced glorious' angel.[20] Ladislaw's sun-ny brightness, the little ripple in his nose which is a preparation for metamorphosis, the way his hair seems to shake out light are set in con-trast (perhaps too easy contrast) with the Saturnian presence of Mr Casaubon, even with Casaubon's own idealized description of himself at the beginning of the book: 'My mind is something like the ghost of an ancient, wandering about the world and trying mentally to construct it as it used to be, in spite of ruin and confusing changes' (2:13). The suc-cession is Apollo's.

Casaubon cannot grasp the ongoing nature of experience, or of knowledge. Imprisoned in his tractate on the Egyptian mysteries, he is incapable of perceiving any relation between the present world and his work. Not only is he ignorant of German scholarship on mythology (which would include the Brothers Grimm's work on folk myth as well as on linguistics),[21] but he is ignorant of the significance of Christian iconography:

Dorothea felt that she was getting quite new notions as to the significance of Madonnas seated under inexplicable canopied thrones with the simple country as a background, and of saints with architectural models in their hands, or knives accidentally wedged in their skulls. Some things which had seemed monstrous to her were gathering intelligibility and even a natural meaning; but all this was apparently a branch of knowledge in which Mr Casaubon had not interested himself. (22:159)

The suggestion is that he thinks it beneath his attention, just as, in a poignant passage, he dismisses the Cupid and Psyche myth as a 'fable' ... 'probably the romantic invention of a literary period,' which 'cannot, I think, to be reckoned as a genuine mythical product' (20:146). The beating of wings, the castle of Amor, night flesh, the travails of Psyche to come again to Love – all these lie outside his imaginative experience. He tabulates; he does not inhabit myth. His method is acquisitive, not radiating. He sees 'the world's ages as a set of box-like partitions without vital connection' (22:157). He is disquieted by the multiplicity of myth: the ways in which differing systems refract meaning at diverse angles, the sense of revelation and yet of incomplete relevance which George Eliot herself explores in her suffusing of experience with mythical analogues.

In contrast to the scientific or artistic imagination which is capable ultimately of 'bathing even the ethereal atoms in its ideally illuminated space' Mr Casaubon has lost the sense of mystery which for George Eliot lies in connections and relations. 'Lost among small closets and winding stairs' he cannot recognize the Ariadne who could deliver him out into sunlight. From his point of view, in their relationship she seems more like a betraying and misleading Cleopatra. In his 'bitter manuscript remarks on other men's notions about the solar deities he had become indifferent to the sunlight' (20:147).

At the beginning of the eighteen-seventies Max Müller's interpretation of myth in terms of solar symbolism was the dominant intellectual reading.[22] George Eliot invokes the system herself within the novel in her treatment of Ladislaw and in the hindsight knowledge with which she judges Casaubon, but she does not allow it to dominate her created world. The scientific imagery ranges far forward beyond any research that Lydgate succeeds in accomplishing. The variety of myth and legend within the book embraces a free-ranging lateral world of meaning beyond Mr Casaubon's awareness. Most important of all, she uses these immanent worlds to indicate that any single interpretation of experience will mislead. The self, to be valid, must stand as *pars pro toto*. The single focus contains; the one candle makes for introspective vision.

Your pier-glass or extensive surface of polished steel made to be rubbed by a house-maid, will be minutely and multitudinously scratched in all directions; but place now against it a lighted candle as a centre of illumination, and lo! the scratches will seem to arrange themselves in a fine series of concentric circles round that little sun. It is demonstrable that the scratches are going everywhere impartially, and it is only your candle which produces the flattering illusion of a concentric arrangement, its light falling with an exclusive optical selection. These things are a parable. (27:194-5)

The maze is what matters. The recurrent imagery of the web suggests simultaneously entanglement and creative order — and beyond them both, the web of human veins and tissue: the being of man.

In *The Lifted Veil* Latimer felt violated not only by his 'prevision of incalculable words and actions' but by the obtrusion into his mind of 'the vagrant, frivolous ideas and emotions of some uninteresting acquaintance.' George Eliot's creativity escapes from the dilemma of determinism by invoking the multiple and the latent. The sense of myriad other lives here becomes a resource rather than a threat. In *Middlemarch* George Eliot sustains our sense of each individual self as worthy of insight, even of inhabiting. She will not yet allow her characters to

escape into liberated futurity as she does at the end of *Daniel Deronda.*
That involves a renewed faith in the generating power of visions, prescience, and tradition — when enriched by being a part of a common
culture founded on race and religion. The aberrant insight and foresight
of *The Lifted Veil* imaged the alienated condition of the artist who can
find no way out of the self. In *Middlemarch* wholeness can be ap-
proached only through relations. The visionary must find expression, if
at all, through the imperfect here and now of ordinary human lots. The
need for mystery, for the sense of other worlds, persists: 'the growing
heritage / That makes completer manhood' is sustained by the outward-
moving scientific imagination, the light that 'turns / To energy of
human fellowship' is shown in myth's illumination of recurrent human
need. Cincinnatus and Caleb Garth are simple kin; Dorothea is in experience no martyr, but the bearer of fruit and flowers. The human
beings in *Middlemarch,* equally with the author and reader in the outer
dialogue, are 'incarnate history.'[23]

NOTES

1   *The George Eliot Letters* Gordon Haight ed (Oxford 1956) III 227. Hereafter
    GEL.
2   GEL V 380 (26 February 1873)
3   GEL III 67. It was published anonymously as 'The Hidden Veil,' in the
    midst of the furore about Liggins, the supposed author of George
    Eliot's novels.
4   GEL V 379 and 380
5   GEL III 41 (31 March 1859)
6   The idea of a future life was a recurrent concern for George Eliot, first ex-
    pressed in the unpublished work of that title which was announced in *The
    Leader,* 18 June 1853. In 1859 she wrote (GEL III 230-1) to M. D'Albert
    that she could not accept 'a superhuman revelation of the Unseen' and
    though feeling sympathy with the idea of future existence: 'my most rooted
    conviction is, that the immediate objects and the proper sphere of all our
    highest emotions are our struggling fellow-men and this earthly existence.'
    When she began work on *Middlemarch* her step-son Thornie was dying,
    and Gordon Haight suggests that at this time her mind dwelt increasingly on
    the idea of a future life: see *George Eliot: A Biography* Gordon S. Haight
    (New York and Oxford 1968) 421.
7   GEL III 60. 'Some readers seem not to have understood, namely — that it
    was in Adam's peasant blood and nurture to believe in this, and that he

narrated it with awed belief to his dying day. That is not a fancy of my own brain, but a matter of observation ...'

8   It is worth remarking the extraordinary number of names which George Eliot created for herself or had attached to her by her intimates: Mary Anne Evans becomes Mary Ann becomes Marian. In writing of herself to M. D'Albert she is Minie. Lewes calls her Polly and Madonna; her stepsons say Mutter and Mother and Madonna; she insists on being called Mrs Lewes, not Miss Evans; she becomes Mrs Cross and George Eliot changes from being a disguise to being a fully synthesising name.

9   See, for example, her Journal, 28 August 1860, where she records 'feeling much depressed just now with self-dissatisfaction and fear that I may not be able to do anything more that is well worth doing.'

10   See her review of Ruskin's *Modern Painters*, volume III, *Westminster Review* 66 (April 1856), and, for example, her essay on Riehl, 'The Natural History of German Life,' *Westminster Review* 66 (July 1856), collected in *Essays of George Eliot* Thomas Pinney ed (London 1963) 266-99: 'art is the nearest thing to life; it is a mode of amplifying experience and extending our contact with our fellow-men beyond the bounds of our personal lot. All the more sacred is the task of the artist when he undertakes to paint the life of the people.' 'The thing for mankind to know is, not what are the motives and influences which the moralist thinks *ought* to act on the labourer or the artisan, but what are the motives and influences which *do* act on him.'

11   See 'A Huxley Echo in *Middlemarch,'* *Notes and Queries* (June 1964) 227.

12   *Modern Painters* IV chapter 7. See the description of Dorothea's hyperaesthetic response (20:143-4).

13   For an illuminating discussion of the uses of science in *Middlemarch* see Michael York Mason, *'Middlemarch* and Science: Problems of Life and Mind,' *Review of English Studies* ns 22 (1971) 151-69. For a discussion of issues of intellectual history, including mythography, in *Middlemarch*, see W.J. Harvey, 'The Intellectual Background of the Novel: Casaubon and Lydgate,' in 'Middlemarch': *Critical Approaches* Barbara Hardy ed (London 1967). For a discussion of the microscope within the novel see, for example, 15:110.

14   'Miss Brooke had that kind of beauty which seems to be thrown into relief by poor dress. Her hand and wrist were so finely formed that she could wear sleeves not less bare of style than those in which the Blessed Virgin appeared to Italian painters' (1:5).

15   *Vita Anskarii*, Bishop Rimbert, c ?880. The account that George Eliot used may have been *Leben der Erzbischöfe Anskar und Rimbert* übersetzt von J.C.M. Laurent (Berlin 1856) or *Leben des heiligen Ansgar* übersetzt von L. Dreves (Paderborn 1864). The latter was prepared for the thousanth anniversary of his death in 1865. The Life is available in an English translation by Charles H. Robinson, a Society for the Propagation of the Gospel in Foreign Parts publication (London 1921). I am indebted to Mr Peter Dronke whose erudition helped me to bring a long search to its conclusion.

16   'The beautiful light round those who were sitting proceeded from [God] Himself and extended like a rainbow. When, then, I had been brought by the men whom I mentioned into the presence of this unending light, where the majesty of Almighty God was revealed to me without need for anyone to explain, and when they and I had offered our united adoration, a most sweet voice, the sound of which was more distinct than all sounds, and which seemed to me to fill the whole world, came forth from the same divine majesty, and addressed me and said, "Go and return to Me crowned with martyrdom." '

17   *Sacred and Legendary Art* (2 volumes, London 1848) I, Introduction xxi and xxii

18   *Sacred and Legendary Art* II 184-9. When naming her heroine George Eliot may well also have had in mind *Hermann und Dorothea*. Note for example the passage from the second canto given in G.H. Lewes' *Life of Goethe* VI 414: 'Overtaking the emigrants, he fell in with a cart drawn by oxen, wherein lay a poor woman beside the infant to which she had just given birth. Leading the oxen was a maiden, *who came towards him with the calm confidence of a generous soul* [my italics] and begged his aid for the poor woman whom she had just assisted in her travail. Touched with pity, and feeling at once that the maiden was the best person to distribute justly the aid he had brought, Hermann gave it all into her hands.' The parallels with Dorothea's personality and function are clear.

19   The whole story is quoted in Charles Kingsley's vigorous and perceptive review essay, *Fraser's Magazine* 39 (1849), where he is discussing the distrust of the imagination and the lack of imaginative food in a Protestant education: 'In the meantime some of the deepest cravings of the human heart have been left utterly unsatisfied ... But in the last generation – and, alas! in this also – little or no proper care has been taken of the love for all which is romantic, marvellous, heroic, which exists in every ingenuous child. Schoolboys ... might ... gloat over the "Seven Champions of Christendom," or Lempriere's gods and goddesses; girls, might, perhaps, be allowed to devour by stealth a few fairy tales or the "Arabian Nights"; but it was only by connivance that their longings were satisfied from the scraps of Moslemism, Paganism – anywhere but from Christianity. Protestantism had nothing to do with the imagination – in fact, it was a question whether reasonable people had any.' Dorothea 'brought up in English and Swiss Puritanism, fed on meagre Protestant histories and on art chiefly of the hand-screen sort' is overwhelmed and at a loss in Rome in the face of its sacred and legendary art.

20   See for example 21:155. In her discussion 'Of the Significance of Colours,' I xlv, Mrs Jameson says of yellow: 'Yellow, or gold, was the symbol of the sun; of the goodness of God, initiation or marriage, faith, or fruitfulness.' He is also compared with Ariel and Shelley, both creatures of light and air.

21   *Kinder und Hausmärchen* (1812-15). In 1819 Jacob Grimm demonstrated the connections between diverse languages. For George Eliot herself

Friedrich de la Motte Fouqué's *Undine* is an element in the portrayal of both Bertha in *The Lifted Veil* and Rosamond in *Middlemarch*. The tradition of cold nature spirits who wed mortals to gain a soul goes back to Paracelsus (Theophrastus von Hohenheim).

22 In 1873 Andrew Lang launched his first attack on Müller's solar mythography with an article in the *Fortnightly Review* on 'Mythology and Fairy Tales.' Müller's *Comparative Mythology* (1856) reorientated all previous thinking about the origin of myths. See also his *Chips from a German Workshop* (4 volumes, London 1867-73). George Eliot met him on at least one occasion. She was reading his *Lectures on the Science of Language* from the early eighteen-sixties on. She speaks in her letters of her enjoyment of his work. His work on metaphor, myth, and the 'disease of language' influenced Ernst Cassirer and still repays study. For a general account of nineteenth century British mythographers see Richard M. Dorson *The British Folklorists, A History* (London 1968).

23 See 'The Natural History of German Life,' *Westminster Review* 66 (1856), reprinted in Pinney *Essays* 287: 'He sees in European society *incarnate history*' (George Eliot's italics).

Index